TOXIC
WARFARE

T0159544

Theodore Karasik

Prepared for the United States Air Force
Approved for public release; distribution unlimited

RAND
Project AIR FORCE

The research reported here was sponsored by the United States Air Force under Contract F49642-01-C-0003. Further information may be obtained from the Strategic Planning Division, Directorate of Plans, Hq USAF.

Library of Congress Cataloging-in-Publication Data

Karasik, Theodore William.
   Toxic warfare / Theodore Karasik.
    p. cm.
   "MR-1572."
   Includes bibliographical references.
   ISBN 0-8330-3207-0
    1. Poisons—War use. 2. Toxins—War use. 3. Hazardous substances—War use.
   4. Biological warfare. 5. Radioactive wastes—War use. 6. Terrorism. I.Title.

   UG447 .K365 2002
   358'.3—dc21

                           2002026562

Cover design by Maritta Tapanainen

RAND is a nonprofit institution that helps improve policy and decisionmaking through research and analysis. RAND® is a registered trademark. RAND's publications do not necessarily reflect the opinions or policies of its research sponsors.

Published 2002 by RAND
1700 Main Street, P.O. Box 2138, Santa Monica, CA 90407-2138
1200 South Hayes Street, Arlington, VA 22202-5050
201 North Craig Street, Suite 202, Pittsburgh, PA 15213-1516
RAND URL: http://www.rand.org/
To order RAND documents or to obtain additional information,
contact Distribution Services: Telephone: (310) 451-7002;
Fax: (310) 451-6915; Email: order@rand.org

Recent events suggest that "toxic warfare"—or the use of inexpensive chemicals and industrial waste in weaponry—is on the rise. Accordingly, this report offers an initial analysis of the extent of the problem by bringing together what is currently known about toxic weapon use. Both state and nonstate actors (including insurgents and terrorists) are using toxic weapons, which provide an attractive asymmetrical option because they are inexpensive, are available in large quantities, are found in urban areas, and, perhaps most significantly, are not entirely secure from theft or diversion. The substances used to make these weapons have thus far been relegated to low-priority status under international law regulating the use of chemical weapons—thereby making it easier for those interested in their use to gain access to them. This report offers historical examples, most drawn from the past decade, to illustrate where and how such weapons have been used. It also examines U.S. operations during toxic warfare and discusses current thinking in the United States about toxic weapons with respect to both military operations and homeland security.

The report should be of interest to those involved in military and civilian crisis response planning. This study was conducted as part of the Strategy and Doctrine Program of RAND's Project AIR FORCE. Comments are welcomed and may be addressed to the author or to the Program Director, Dr. Ted Harshberger. The cutoff date for this research was January 2002.

PROJECT AIR FORCE

Project AIR FORCE, a division of RAND, is the Air Force federally funded research and development center (FFRDC) for studies and analyses. It provides the Air Force with independent analyses of policy alternatives affecting the development, employment, combat readiness, and support of current and future air and space forces. Research is performed in four programs: Aerospace Force Development; Manpower, Personnel, and Training; Resource Management; and Strategy and Doctrine.

CONTENTS

TABLES

In recent years, there appears to be an increased interest in weapons that incorporate chemicals and industrial wastes that are both inexpensive and relatively easy to acquire. Such "toxic weapons" provide a means for hostile state or nonstate actors to improve their capabilities within the context of asymmetrical warfare. In basic terms, toxic warfare refers to the use of chemicals or industrial waste to harm or alter the behavior of an opponent during military operations. Toxic warfare does not, however, require the use of traditional weapons; it can also involve the release of chemicals into the environment (e.g., from industrial manufacturing or waste sites). A preliminary review of incidents involving toxic weapons suggests that such weapons merit greater attention as part of military and civilian crisis response planning.

WHAT ARE TOXIC WEAPONS?

In contrast to chemical weapons, which involve the use of banned substances such as the nerve agents sarin and soman, toxic weapons are made from materials that are usually readily (and legally) available in connection with industrial operations. The most common types of hazardous materials used in toxic weapons are irritants, choking agents, flammable industrial gases, water supply contaminants, oxidizers, chemical asphyxiants, incendiary gases and liquids, industrial compounds, and organophosphate pesticides. Various forms of toxic waste (e.g., petroleum spills, smoke, refuse, sewage, and medical waste) can also be used in toxic warfare.

Abundant sources of industrial materials and waste are available for use in toxic warfare. Although large industrial facilities are an obvious source of concern, other common urban locations, such as airports, college laboratories, and even garden-supply warehouses, pose risks as well. Illegal chemical and toxic waste sites are another potentially significant source of toxic warfare materials.

Toxic warfare can be used by both state and nonstate actors to achieve a number of objectives. Toxic warfare can cause casualties among opposing militaries by incapacitating and, in some cases, killing the adversary. Toxic warfare can also halt or force delays in military logistics flows or operations and can disrupt the functioning of the urban infrastructure through contamination or corrosion. Toxic weapons can, moreover, derive power from the uncertainty that stems from their potential use. Toxic substances often represent an unknown threat, and the level of uncertainty surrounding the potential damage these substances *might* cause can increase their impact even when little or no physical harm has been done.

RECENT USE OF TOXIC WEAPONS

There have been many incidents of toxic warfare in recent years. During the Gulf War, retreating Iraqi forces intentionally caused the release of crude petroleum from field production facilities and ignited the oil to slow advancing coalition forces—the only time U.S. operations have faced a toxic attack. During the Balkan wars, Serbian forces attacked a Croatian Petrochemia facility that stored large quantities of anhydrous ammonia and a variety of other potentially hazardous chemicals. From 1993 to 1995, the facility was attacked six times with rockets, bombs, artillery, and mortars. Serbian forces also intentionally targeted a pesticide production facility at Sisak and a natural gas refinery in Ivanic. During the siege of Muslim forces in Tuzla by the Serbs, the Muslims threatened to release large quantities of chlorine gas from railroad tank cars under their control despite the large number of friendly casualties that would have resulted. Other toxic incidents have occurred in Chechnya, Sri Lanka, and the Middle East.

Some new trends in toxic warfare also seem to be emerging. For example, toxic weapons seem to be used more frequently in conjunction with increasingly complex forms of organization, training, and equipment, including that represented by Al-Qaeda and Osama bin Laden. Another trend concerns increased opportunism in the use or combination of toxic substances. Those who use toxic weapons seek to create uncertainty by exploiting whatever opportunities are available to bend the definition of chemical warfare and conventional conflict through their choice of toxic materials and tactics.

TOXIC THREATS IN EXPEDITIONARY SETTINGS

Although U.S. military forces have not yet faced repeated threats from toxic weapons, that possibility clearly exists, particularly in light of the wide availability of toxic materials. One such threat arises from toxic smoke in the field of operations, which can be used to cause confusion, impair vision, and disrupt military operations. Water supplies in areas of operations are vulnerable to both intentional and accidental contamination. Toxic waste poses another threat. The U.S. military is currently seeking to improve its ability to respond to toxic warfare by updating military field manuals and related documents to address the issue of organizing, training, and equipping for such warfare.

At the same time, however, the level of threat that toxic weapons represent remains to be determined. Should toxic warfare be considered a mere nuisance or a threat of strategic concern? Although it is impossible to know how extensively toxic weapons will be used in the future, there are several reasons for concluding that toxic warfare merits serious consideration as part of future planning strategies.

- **The United States is not immediately aware of the location of toxic threats.** In future operations, it is possible that an entire area of operations could be contaminated with toxic waste. Although the identification of specific threats is a painstaking process, U.S. forces will need to improve their knowledge of the locations of both legal and illegal sources of toxic waste.

- **At the operational level, U.S. forces currently have no tailored response to toxic warfare in doctrine.** In particular, the U.S. military will need to resolve at the doctrinal level the trade-off between force protection and mobility/agility. Put another way, to what extent does the potential for toxic warfare require that chemical kits, protective clothing, cleanup materials, and the like be carried on operations if doing so would impede the mobility and agility of the forces?

- **The use of toxic weapons has implications for U.S. military lift and logistics.** As base security becomes more critical to operations, the vulnerability of key logistics sites has emerged as an important issue. Many sites are vulnerable to toxic attack, including ports, airfields, and related fixed sites that serve as choke points. Support staging areas as well as rail and road networks are also potential targets, as are intermediate and infrastructure logistics bases. Procedures will be needed to address these threats.

- **At the tactical level, U.S. armed forces may not be ready for toxic warfare.** The Office of the Secretary of Defense has found a number of problems associated with preparation for toxic warfare as a subset of a nuclear, biological, or chemical attack. For example, toxic vapors often hug the ground, an issue that is not addressed in some scenarios. Air Force programs also require additional policy and guidance, an integrated training and exercise program, and first-responder equipment for addressing toxic attacks.

- **Cleanup from a toxic attack may pose a difficult challenge.** The decontamination of aircraft presents an especially difficult challenge, as demonstrated by the oil-laden rain encountered by coalition forces during the Gulf War. Decontamination procedures will need to address fixed sites as well as cargo and equipment.

TOXIC THREATS IN THE UNITED STATES

Toxic warfare is a threat not just for U.S. forces engaged in military operations but also for civilians within the United States. This risk is increased by the wide availability of toxic materials throughout the United States, together with the proximity of industrial operations to large urban centers.

At the forefront of toxic warfare in the United States are the first responders, whose mission is to respond immediately in the event of a crisis or disaster. First responders include personnel from medical, law enforcement (or security), fire/rescue, hazardous material

(HAZMAT), and explosive ordnance disposal organizations. U.S. domestic responders are in the process of organizing, training, and equipping to counter potential attacks.

Other domestic capabilities, however, need to be improved as well. Currently, for example, there is no consistent approach toward burden sharing among agencies, particularly with regard to treating casualties. Internet connectivity in many hospitals remains poor, with only 25 percent of laboratories up to federal standards for access to and dissemination of information. Moreover, in the event of multiple toxic attacks, the scope of response needed could overwhelm local resources.

Military and civilian crisis response preparedness efforts must also be better coordinated. The U.S. military possesses chemical weapon prevention and cleanup expertise that is applicable to homeland security. Civilian crisis response personnel can for their part provide expertise in areas such as HAZMAT. Additional opportunities to share information and coordinate efforts need to be identified.

Finally, the risks associated with toxic warfare—both for expeditionary forces and within the United States—must be better understood. Planning for military operations and civilian crisis response requires a detailed understanding of the benefits and costs associated with various options for countering toxic weapons. While this report is meant to fill some of the gaps in understanding surrounding toxic weapons, a quantitative risk assessment should be considered as a means of providing a more thorough evaluation of the problem.

ACKNOWLEDGMENTS

The contents of this report are the result of discussions with colleagues at the Armed Forces Medical Intelligence Center, the Air Mobility Command, Lawrence Livermore National Laboratory, the Monterey Institute of International Studies, the Central Intelligence Agency, the Defense Intelligence Agency, the National Ground Intelligence Center, and the U.S. Transportation Command (TRANSCOM). RAND colleagues Ted Harshberger, Eric Larson, Derek Eaton, Jed Peters, William O'Malley, Les Dishman, Richard Bancroft, and Leroy Reyes also contributed commentary to early ideas and evolving thought as well as useful primary and secondary sources. Special thanks go to Kristin Leuschner, who edited and critiqued the original draft.

ACRONYMS

AFMIC	Armed Forces Medical Intelligence Center
APOD	Aerial port of debarkation
C^2	Command and control
C^4I	Command, control, communications, computers, and intelligence
CBRN	Chemical, biological, radiological, and nuclear
CBW	Chemical and biological weapon
CINC	Commander in chief
CONUS	Continental United States
CWC	Chemical Weapons Convention
ELN	Army of National Liberation (Colombia)
EOD	Explosive ordnance disposal
FAE	Fuel air explosive
FARC	Revolutionary Armed Forces of Colombia
FM	Field Manual
HAZMAT	Hazardous material
HQ AFCESA	Headquarters, Air Force Civil Engineer Support Agency

IO	Information operations
JP	Joint Publication
KTO	Kuwaiti theater of operations
LPG	Liquefied petroleum gas
LTTE	Liberation Tigers of Tamil Eelam
MIC	Methyl isocyanate
NBC	Nuclear, biological, and chemical
OSD	Office of the Secretary of Defense
PCB	Polychlorinated biphenyl
PKK	Kurdish Workers Party
POE	Port of embarkation
PSYOP	Psychological operations
SBCCOM	Soldier and Biological Chemical Command (U.S. Army)
TRANSCOM	Transportation Command
UNPROFOR	United Nations Protection Force
USACMLS	U.S. Army Chemical School
WMD	Weapons of mass destruction

Chapter One

INTRODUCTION

In recent years, there would appear to be an increased interest in weapons that incorporate inexpensive, relatively easy-to-acquire chemicals and industrial wastes. Such "toxic weapons" might take the form of a rocket containing insecticide or several barrels of toxic chemicals left in an adversary's path to force the diversion of troops. To date, however, instances of toxic warfare have not been subjected to extensive analysis, largely because greater interest has been manifested in more sophisticated forms of chemical warfare, including the use of weapons of mass destruction (WMD) and the development of nuclear, biological, and chemical (NBC) doctrine.[1]

A preliminary review of incidents involving toxic weapons suggests that they merit greater attention, especially because of the threat they pose within the context of asymmetrical warfare. Asymmetrical strategies focus on attacking an adversary's points of vulnerability by

---

[1]See Jean Pascal Zanders, "Assessing the Risk of Chemical and Biological Weapons Proliferation to Terrorists," *Nonproliferation Review*, Fall 1999, pp. 17–34; Raymond A. Zilinskas, "The Threat of Bioterrorism," Center for Nonproliferation Studies briefing, August 3, 1998, available at http://cns.miis.edu/iiop/cnsdata; Al J. Venter, "Biological Warfare: The Poor Man's Atomic Bomb," *Jane's Intelligence Review*, Vol. 11, No. 3, March 1, 1999, p. 42; Malcolm Dando, "Discriminating Bio-Weapons Could Target Ethnic Groups," *International Defense Review*, Vol. 30, No. 3, March 1, 1997, p. 77; Gert G. Harigel, *Chemical and Biological Weapons: Use in Warfare, Impact on Society and Environment*, Carnegie Endowment for International Peace, available at http://www.ceip.org/files/publications/Harigelreport.asp?p=8; *Chemical Warfare: A Burning Issue—Project on Insurgency, Terrorism and Security*, available at http://paladin-san-francisco.com/libgas03.htm; Jonathan B. Tucker (ed.), *Toxic Terror: Assessing Terrorist Use of Chemical and Biological Weapons*, Cambridge, MA: MIT Press, 2000; and Graham Spearson, "Strategic and Security Issues: Forbidden, Not Forgotten," *International Defense Review*, Vol. 30, No. 3, March 1, 1997, available at Intelink.

increasing the level of threat in areas in which that adversary is least prepared. Asymmetrical tactics seek means of catching the enemy off guard, and they do so using unexpected—as well as typically inexpensive and easily available—means of attack.

Toxic weapons provide an opportunity for hostile state or nonstate actors to increase their asymmetrical capabilities. The materials for toxic warfare are ubiquitous, particularly in industrialized nations such as the United States. The number of such attacks seems to be on the increase, and the potential exists for more frequent and more lethal uses of such weapons in the future. This risk can increase to the extent that U.S. troops are deployed to unstable, unsafe areas in which toxic materials are readily available.

This study attempts to fill some of the gaps in our understanding of toxic weapons in asymmetrical warfare. Toward this goal, it first examines the scope of the risks these weapons pose. It then describes some recent incidents involving toxic warfare and proceeds to discuss the nature of the risk both to U.S. expeditionary forces and to the U.S. homeland.

RECENT EXAMPLES OF TOXIC WARFARE

The manner in which industrial chemicals may be intentionally used as toxic weapons can be briefly illustrated through some examples drawn from the Gulf War and the Balkan conflict. In 1990, retreating Iraqi forces intentionally caused the release of crude petroleum from field production facilities and ignited the oil in efforts to slow advancing coalition forces. In the mid-1990s, the Balkan conflict involved frequent attacks on chemical production facilities. From 1993 to 1995, for example, Serbian forces launched six attacks on a Petrochemia facility near Kutina, Croatia, that stored large quantities of anhydrous ammonia as well as a variety of other potentially hazardous chemicals; these attacks involved rockets, bombs, artillery, and mortars. Serbian forces are also known to have targeted a pesticide production facility at Sisak and a natural gas refinery in Ivanic. Although none of these attempts was wholly successful, subsequent U.S. modeling efforts indicated that if the attacks had destroyed existing stored chemical containers, lethal concentrations of chemicals would likely have spread over a wide area. Toxic weapons were also used against the Serbs, such as when Muslim forces in

Tuzla threatened the use of chemicals in efforts to hold off a Serbian attack against the city. These forces vowed to release large quantities of chlorine gas from railroad tank cars if the city was assaulted—despite the large number of friendly casualties that would have resulted from such an action.

THE UBIQUITY OF RAW MATERIALS FOR TOXIC WEAPONS

Although the threat posed by toxic weaponry may in some cases be little more than a nuisance, in other cases it can have catastrophic results. Indeed, the fact that some acts of toxic warfare have been ineffective should not be used as evidence that the threat from these weapons is low, especially in light of the ubiquity of toxic substances both within the United States and worldwide. The relatively easy access to such materials, when combined with their low cost and the low security often associated with storage facilities, makes them a potentially attractive and highly available option for asymmetrical warfare. Industrialized nations are home to thousands of facilities and sites that manufacture, use, or transport toxic substances; these include oil and gas installations, extended pipelines, refineries, and chemical shipping facilities.[2] At the same time, chemicals useful for toxic warfare can be obtained almost anywhere in the world. Existing stored chemicals—including those found on military sites—can easily be made to serve as "weapons of opportunity."

The notion of opportunism is central to this discussion. A manufacturing capability is not required in order for industrial chemicals to be used as weapons. In fact, these substances need not even be shaped into anything resembling a traditional weapon in order to be effective. In some cases, toxic warfare could occur as a "side effect" of more traditional military operations, such as when damage to industrial facilities from military operations leads to a catastrophic chemical release. Indeed, the very presence of such facilities can threaten military operations in urban areas, which could be affected if, for example, an electrical power interruption or an improper facility shutdown were to cause a chemical release. Such events are common during complex emergencies, armed conflicts, and post-

---

[2]See "Forced to Take a Lead on Hazardous Materials," *Jane's International Police Review*, January 1, 2000, available at Intelink.

conflict reconstitution periods. The key point is that while toxic warfare is typically initiated by a deliberate act, it can also result when adversaries exploit the opportunities presented by accidental toxic releases and the ubiquity of toxic substances.

THE IMPACT OF TOXIC WEAPONS

Toxic warfare is used by state and nonstate actors to achieve military and political goals. On one level, toxic warfare can cause casualties among opposing militaries. It can incapacitate and in some cases kill the adversary, although the latter objective is not necessarily the primary motivation for its use. Toxic warfare can also halt or force delays in military logistics flows or operations. Similarly, it can disrupt the functioning of the urban infrastructure and create panic among the citizenry. Yet much of the power of toxic weapons lies in the uncertainty associated with their potential use. Toxic substances often represent an unknown threat, and the level of uncertainty surrounding the potential damage these substances *might* cause—be it to soldiers in transit, to the civilian population, or to urban infrastructure and military logistics—can increase their effect even in cases in which little or no physical harm has occurred. Thus, while more conventional types of weapons might cause greater levels of collateral damage and can be more accurately targeted, toxic weapons are useful in asymmetrical warfare precisely because they use relatively small amounts of available chemicals or industrial waste to create what seems to be—and sometimes is—a disproportionately large and potentially devastating threat.

Toxic warfare remains a possibility within the United States in large part because of the size of the U.S. industrial infrastructure, which makes greater use of toxic chemicals and produces more industrial waste than any other country in the world. The quantity of chemicals alone provides terrorists with many potential opportunities to use toxic weapons to scare, maim, and kill. The possibility of toxic warfare is especially likely during complex emergencies and conflict.

ABOUT THIS REPORT

This study provides a qualitative overview of the threat posed by toxic weapons and identifies key vulnerabilities faced by the United

States and the U.S. military, particularly the U.S. Air Force. Because the analysis is drawn entirely from unclassified sources, it cannot offer a detailed analysis of the intelligence requirements for toxic warfare. Nor does the report seek to provide a quantitative assessment of the risks associated with toxic weapons. While such an effort may prove useful and even necessary in helping the U.S. military determine how great an effort should be directed toward toxic weapons, it was beyond the scope of this study.

The remainder of the report focuses on several issues related to toxic warfare. Chapter Two explains the composition and sources of toxic weapons as well as their potential for harm. Chapter Three analyzes the use of toxic weapons by state and nonstate actors over the past decade and considers the potential for escalated use. Chapter Four focuses on the threat to U.S. forces that are engaged in expeditionary operations, particularly the U.S. Air Force. Finally, Chapter Five considers the nature of the threat to the U.S. homeland.

Chapter Two

WHAT ARE TOXIC WEAPONS?

If we are to analyze the potential threat toxic weapons pose, we must first look in more detail at the nature of toxic weapons, the sources of materials for those weapons, and the type of damage they can cause. This chapter addresses each of these issues in turn.

THE COMPONENTS OF TOXIC WARFARE

Put simply, toxic warfare refers to the use of chemicals or industrial waste to harm or alter the behavior of an opponent during military operations.[1] Toxic warfare does not require the use of weapons per se; while toxic substances may be incorporated into traditional weaponry, such warfare can also involve the release of chemicals into the environment (e.g., from industrial manufacturing or waste sites) without the use of any traditional weapons. Toxic warfare typically involves the use of inert chemicals that in some cases produce immediate, mild health effects. These conditions cannot, however, spread without direct exposure to the substances, which are relatively nonpersistent in the environment. In contrast to chemical weapons, which can involve the use of banned substances such as the nerve agents sarin and soman, toxic weapons are made from materials that are usually readily (and legally) available in connection with industrial operations.

---

[1]Dust agents are also part of toxic warfare in that toxic materials can absorb substances and carry the agent toward its intended target site depending on the time of day or night, the ground and air temperature, and weather patterns at the site of use.

Among the most common types of hazardous materials are the following:

- Irritants (acids, ammonia, acrylates, aldehydes, and isocyanates);

- Choking agents (chlorine, hydrogen sulfide, and phosgene);

- Flammable industrial gases (acetone, alkenes, alkyl halides, and amines);

- Water supply contaminants (aromatic hydrocarbons, benzene, etc.);

- Oxidizers capable of increasing the danger of explosions (oxygen, butadiene, and peroxides);

- Chemical asphyxiants (aniline, nitrile, and cyanide compounds);

- Incendiary gases (compressed isobutene, liquefied natural gas, and propane);

- Incendiary liquids (liquid hydrocarbons, gasoline, and diesel and jet fuel);

- Industrial compounds that act much like blister agents (dimethyl sulfate); and

- Organophosphate pesticides that can act as low-grade nerve agents.

Various forms of toxic waste (which may include petroleum spills, smoke, refuse, sewage, and medical waste) can also be used in toxic warfare. All these substances can contribute in varying degrees to a state or nonstate actor's asymmetrical capability.[2]

------

[2]Joint Publication (JP) 3-11 defines industrial chemicals as chemicals developed or manufactured in industrial operations or research by industry, government, or academia. These chemicals are not primarily manufactured for the specific purpose of producing human casualties or rendering equipment, facilities, or areas dangerous for human use. Hydrogen cyanide, cyanogen chloride, phosgene, and chloropicrin are industrial chemicals that can also be military chemical agents. This term and its definition are approved for inclusion in the next edition of JP 1-02. See *Joint Doctrine for Operations in Nuclear, Biological, and Chemical (NBC) Environments*, Washington, D.C., Joint Publication 3-11, July 11, 2000.

The Chemical Weapons Convention (CWC) regulates the use of chemical substances in warfare, including more traditional chemical weapons as well as substances used to make toxic weapons. Article 2, paragraph 1, of the CWC defines "chemical weapons" as

(a)   Toxic chemicals and their precursors, except where intended for purposes not prohibited under this Convention, as long as the types and quantities are consistent with such purposes;

(b)   Munitions and devices, specifically designed to cause death or other harm through the toxic properties of those toxic chemicals specified in subparagraph (a), which would be released as a result of the employment of such munitions and devices; [and]

(c)   Any equipment specifically designed for use directly in connection with the employment of munitions and devices specified in subparagraph (b).

Many of the substances used in toxic weapons are found on Schedule 3 of the CWC.[3]   While Schedule 1 of the CWC focuses on superlethal

---

[3]Schedule 1 lists three families of nerve agents: the sarin, soman, and GF family; the tabun family; and the VX family. Nerve agents are organophosphorous chemicals of very high toxicity. The first nerve agent, tabun, was discovered in 1936 during a search for better pesticides. Nerve agents act by inhibiting the enzyme acetylcholinesterase, thus preventing the enzyme from destroying the neurotransmitter acetylcholine after it has transmitted a nerve signal to a muscle. The muscle will then remain contracted—i.e., in cramp. Few or no peaceful uses have yet been identified for any members of the three listed nerve agent families.

Schedule 1 includes two families of nerve agent precursors and two individual nerve agent precursor chemicals. Mustard agents and lewisites cause wounds resembling burns and blisters. They can also cause severe damage to the eyes, respiratory system, and internal organs. Schedule 1 includes 15 agents of this type: nine sulfur mustards, three nitrogen mustards, and three lewisites. Mustard gas was discovered in 1822 and was used extensively during World War I. In the 1930s it was used against Abyssinia and China and in the 1980s against Iran. A considerable part of the present-day stockpile of chemical weapons to be destroyed under the convention consists of mustard agent in bulk form and in filled munitions.

Two toxins have been included in Schedule 1: ricin and saxitoxin. Both have been studied for possible use as chemical weapons. Ricin is a protein that is formed in the seeds of the widely cultivated castor oil plant, from which it can be extracted. It is more toxic than nerve agents on a weight basis and acts by blocking the body's syn-

weapons that involve nerve agents and Schedule 2 includes dual-use (both industrial and military) chemicals (typically of limited use), Schedule 3 focuses on chemicals that can be legally used in industrial processes. Schedule 3 chemicals tend to be easier to obtain than those listed in Schedules 1 and 2 and can be employed for destructive purposes. Typically they have also been less widely emphasized than those found in Schedules 1 and 2.

One of the greatest threats from Schedule 3 toxins comes when substances are combined. The result can be a weapon-grade substance such as phosgene, cyanogen chloride, hydrogen cyanide, and chloropicrin. Each of these chemicals has a legitimate industrial use but also poses a threat in toxic warfare. Phosgene is a gas used as an intermediate in the preparation of many organic chemicals, including agrochemicals, and was used in chemical weapons during World War I. Inhalation can be fatal, but exposure may not be noticed immediately. Cyanogen chloride and hydrogen cyanide are both important synthetic intermediates; hydrogen cyanide has also been used as a pesticide. Both can block cell respiration, and high concentrations can be fatal within minutes. Chloropicrin is a soil sterilant, grain

---

thesis of proteins. Ricin is being studied as a possible chemotherapeutic agent for the treatment of leukemia and liver cancer. Saxitoxin is a complex organic chemical synthesized by a blue-green algae species. These algae provide food for mussels, which accumulate the toxin. The toxin acts on the nervous system. One milligram can eventually kill a human being. Higher doses may be lethal within 15 minutes. Saxitoxin is used as a biochemical research tool.

Schedule 2 agents are dual-use chemicals of limited use. There are three toxic chemicals. Amiton is an organophosphorous insecticide that was first synthesized around 1950. Today it is considered too toxic for use in agriculture. PFIB, short for perfluoroisobutylene, is a gas that is formed as a by-product during the production of some perfluorinated polymers, such as Teflon. It has no commercial application. Its toxicity is similar to that of phosgene (see below). BZ has earlier been weaponized as an incapacitating agent to be disseminated as aerosolized solid particles. It is widely used in minute quantities as a biochemical research tool and is also an intermediate in the production of a pharmaceutical. Finally, Schedule 2 includes a considerable number of precursors to nerve agents, mustard gas, lewisites, and BZ. All chemicals containing a phosphorus atom with one attached methyl, ethyl or propyl group are included (with one exception: the pesticide fonophos).

Schedule 3 includes phosgene (carbonyl dichloride), cyanogen chloride, hydrogen cyanide, and chloropicrin (trichloronitromethane). Precursors are phosphorus oxychloride, phosphorus trichloride, phosphorus pentachloride, trimethyl phosphite, triethyl phosphite, dimethyl phosphite, diethyl phosphite, sulfur monochloride, sulfur dichloride, thionyl chloride, ethyldiethanolamine, methyldiethanolamine, and triethanolamine.

disinfectant, and synthetic intermediate. Exposure can cause severe irritation and lacrimation.

Although Schedule 3 chemicals are not considered nerve agents either by international law or by chemical treaty, Schedule 3 includes seven nerve agent precursors. Examples include phosphorus oxychloride and phosphorus trichloride, which have extensive applications in the chemical industry, including insecticide production and chlorination. Three sulfur mustard and three nitrogen mustard precursors are listed on Schedule 3, including triethanolamine, which has several uses ranging from the production of surface-active chemicals to use as a solvent. Sulfur monochloride serves as a chlorinating agent in the production of dyes and pesticides and is also used for cold vulcanization of rubber and as a polymerization catalyst for vegetable oils.

As these examples suggest, toxic weapons can have lethal potential—although, as will be shown later, they need not be lethal in order to be effective.

SOURCES OF TOXIC SUBSTANCES

One of the most important features of toxic weapons is the ready availability of the substances used to create them. There are abundant sources of industrial materials and waste for use in toxic warfare. In fact, chemical waste is likely to be found in some form and quantity at any industrial site. Unprocessed laboratory solvents, for example, pose a risk of toxic exposure, especially if they enter into the water supply. The risk of toxic exposure is significant because chemical production sources and stockpiles are frequently stored in drums and tanks located near inhabited areas. Industrial chemicals that are released as vapors can pose an additional risk because they tend to remain concentrated in locations downwind from the release point and can accumulate in low-lying areas such as valleys, ravines, and man-made underground structures. Table 2.1 lists the major industrial sources of chemical toxins.

While large industrial facilities are obviously sources of major concern for toxic weaponry, other common urban locations pose risks as well. Urban areas that contain toxic materials include airports, col-

Table 2.1

Potential Sources of Chemical Toxins for State and Nonstate Use

Paint formulation and organic chemical producers
Production of pesticides and wood preservatives
Manufacturing plants and smelting industries
Agricultural fumigants, industrial wastes, and pharmaceutical wastes
Lead, mercury, and cadmium-nickel battery manufacture
Textile mills, cosmetics manufacturing, dyeing and tanning industries
Petroleum refining

SOURCE: George A. Alexander, "Ecoterrorism and Nontraditional Military Threats," *Military Medicine*, Vol. 165, No. 1, January 2000, p. 3.

lege laboratories, and even garden-supply warehouses.[4] The most common risks are associated with gases, especially the irritants chlorine, sulfur dioxide, ammonia, and hydrogen chloride. Table 2.2 shows the most common locations and sources of toxic materials in urban areas.

Another potentially major source of materials for toxic warfare lies in the illegal chemical and toxic waste sites—both industrial and medical—that can be found throughout North America, Europe, the Middle East, and likely East Asia. Millions of tons of toxic waste are transported each year by both organized and nonorganized criminal networks into poorer, urbanized centers in areas of conflict and crisis.[5] Because criminals seek to avoid waste disposal fees, they typically select remote areas to deposit their illegal toxic shipments, thereby making it easy for these materials to be diverted by state or nonstate actors for other uses—including military tactics and operations.[6] Increasingly, these wastes are being transported to

---

[4]Annual waste production is discussed in Gert G. Harigel, *The Concept of Weapons of Mass Destruction: Chemical and Biological Weapons, Use in Warfare, Impact on Society and Environment*, presented at the Conference on Biosecurity and Bioterrorism, Istituto Diplomatico "Mario Toscano," Rome, Italy, September 18–19, 2000, p. 10.

[5]See John Dean, "Organized Crime Versus the Environment," *Jane's International Police Review*, January 1, 2000, available at Intelink; and Christoph Hilz, *The International Toxic Waste Trade*, New York: Van Nostrand Reinhold, 1992.

[6]See "Forced to Take a Lead on Hazardous Materials," January 1, 2000; Mark Galeotti, "Crimes of the New Millennium," *Jane's Intelligence Review*, August 1, 2000, available

Table 2.2

Locations of Toxic Materials in Urban Areas Available to State and Nonstate Actors

Location	Toxic Materials
Airports	Aviation gasoline, jet fuel
Farm and garden-supply warehouses	Pesticides
Barge terminals	Bulk petroleum and chemicals
College laboratories	Organic chemicals, radioactive material
Electronics manufacturers	Arsine, arsenic trichloride
Food processing and storage areas	Ammonia
Glass and mirror plants	Fluorine, hydrofluoric acid
Pipelines and propane storage tanks	Ammonia, methane, and propane
Plastic manufacturers	Isocyanates, cyanide compounds
Landscaping businesses	Ricin
Medical facilities	Radioactive isotopes, mercury, waste
Inorganic chemical plants	Chlorine
Hard rock ore mines	Potassium and sodium cyanide
Pesticide plants	Organophosphate pesticides
Petroleum storage tanks	Gasoline, diesel fuel
Photographic supply distributors	Cyanides, heavy metals
Rail and trucking lines, chemical manufacturing plants	Anhydrous ammonia; sulfuric, phosphoric, and hydrochloric acids; flammable liquids; chlorine; peroxides; and other industrial gases
Power stations and transformers	Polychlorinated biphenyls (PCBs)

SOURCE: *The Infantryman's Guide to Modern Urban Combat,* Field Manual (FM) 90-10-1, Q-2 (coordinating draft), July 1, 2000 (hereafter referred to as FM 90-10-1).

unstable areas. In Somalia and in the Levant, for example, illegal toxic waste transfers measuring in the hundreds of tons occur alongside military operations.[7] Eventually the two may intersect, creating a toxic combat environment that affects the U.S. Air Force and other U.S. services.

---

at Intelink; and Mark Galeotti, "The New World of Organized Crime," *Jane's Intelligence Review*, September 1, 2000, available at Intelink.

[7]The Israeli transfer to Jordan involved 500 tons of toxic material. See Ghassan Joha, "Israel's Bid to Dump Toxic Waste in Jordan Foiled," *The Star*, November 30, 2000, accessed from FBIS-IAP-20001130000091. For more on illegal toxic dumping, see Svend Soyland, *Criminal Organizations and Crimes Against the Environment: A Desktop Study*, Turin, Italy: United National Interregional Crime and Justice Research Institute, June 2000.

THE IMPACT OF TOXIC WARFARE

There are three broad categories of effects associated with toxic warfare: health hazards, damage to or contamination of military or civilian infrastructure, and psychological effects resulting from the actual or threatened use of toxic substances.

In assessing the potential human health hazards or risks from exposure to toxic weapons, we must consider the form of the substance released (solid, liquid, or gas) as well as its innate toxicity and the nature of the exposure (e.g., how much of the chemical was released and whether the person was exposed through inhalation, ingestion, etc.).[8] For humans, the most extreme health effects typically occur as a result of exposure to gases. The irritants chlorine, sulfur dioxide, and hydrogen chloride all have relatively high toxicity when inhaled. In addition, combustibles such as the polymer intermediate vinyl acetate present extreme fire hazards. In the 1970s, the latter compound was responsible for a large, potentially dangerous vapor release in a major metropolitan area; the explosion involved a 30,000-gallon-capacity tank as well as 21 other tanks with chemical substances. The greatest threat to people comes from off-gases, which form from the oxidation of modern plastics and their monomers. Vinyl chloride, carbon monoxide, and hydrogen cyanide, for example, contribute to making phosgene upon burning. As many as half of the deaths attributed to smoke inhalation are actually due to poisonous off-gases released during fires.

The lethality of off-gases was apparent in the 1984 disaster in Bhopal, India, in which a disgruntled employee mixed water into methyl isocyanate (MIC), a chemical intermediate used in the synthesis of carbamate pesticide (sevin). The local inhabitants who gathered around the plant to watch the disaster unfold inhaled the deadly gases released from the mixture of water and MIC and were among the first of more than 3800 fatalities. Although most carbamate pesticides manufactured in Western countries today do not call for large vol-

---

[8]D. J. Rodier and M. G. Zeeman, "Ecological Risk Assessment," in L. G. Cockerham and B. S. Shane, *Basic Environmental Toxicology*, Boca Raton, FL: CRC Press, 1994, pp. 581–604; E. B. Overton, W. D. Sharpe, and P. Roberts, "Toxicity of Petroleum" in *Basic Environmental Toxicology*, pp. 133–156; and P. A. Reinhardt and J. G. Gordon, *Infectious and Medical Waste Management*, Chelsea, MI: Lewis Publishers, 1991.

umes of MIC on-site, MIC is typically transported to the sites during the production process. In addition, other chemicals that are typically kept on-site at Western industrial facilities (e.g., ammonia and phosgene) could potentially result in a catastrophic release of a magnitude similar to that of the Bhopal incident.[9] The impact of such catastrophic releases could involve thousands of individuals, resulting in health effects ranging from minor lung and skin irritation to death.

In addition to causing health effects, toxic substances can be used by state and nonstate actors against civilian and military symbols and infrastructure. Toxic warfare can render infrastructure targets unfit for occupation or use by humans and can also damage structures through corrosion. State and nonstate actors can use toxic warfare against civilian and military building and facilities, population centers, command-and-control (C^2) facilities, and logistical lines. Civilian targets include national monuments, public gathering places, conveyances, and energy and water facilities. Military targets include fixed formations such as bases or troop emplacements and mobile targets such as convoys, columns, and shipping. When used against military targets, toxic weapons can interrupt operations by forcing an opponent to change planning and deployment options on short notice. Other civilian and military targets include military bases, airfields, government and civilian buildings, oil and gas pipelines, pumping stations, refineries, and water supplies as well as transportation infrastructure such as highways and bridges.[10]

Toxic weapons also have the potential for use in psychological operations. The presence of toxic materials or even the possibility of their intended use can result in avoidance, uncertainty, fear, panic, and a host of other reactions in the population—even when the actual physical damage stemming from their use is limited. The extent

---

[9]Derived from interviews with Monterey Institute of International Studies researcher Eric Croddy, 2000–2001.

[10]Water supplies provide an interesting example of the confusion that can result from understanding the difference between a biological and toxic attack. Although the commanders in chief (CINCs) treat water security with stringent security measures, an outright attack is difficult to assess, treat, and counter. See Al J. Venter, "Poisoned Chalice Poses Problems: The Terrorist Threat to the World's Water," *International Defense Review*, Vol. 32, No. 1, January 1, 1999, p. 57.

of psychological effects from toxic warfare is to a large extent unknown, and the unclassified sources reviewed for this report do not provide sufficient evidence to warrant many conclusions in this area. Given the potential for toxic weapons to cause serious harm, however, it is likely that even less toxic substances could be perceived as posing a potentially lethal danger—particularly when the composition of the substances used in such weapons is not known, as is often the case. It is likely that the uncertainty surrounding the use of many toxic weapons will play to the advantage of those who use them.

Such uncertainties are in fact a key feature of toxic weapons and constitute one of the reasons it is difficult to plan a response to their use. An individual act of toxic warfare could be lethal or could be a mere nuisance. Yet the extent of a toxic weapon's impact cannot always be known immediately or even for some time after an attack. For example, there is no question that a weapon incorporating medical waste would have a much smaller relative impact (e.g., five cases of HIV or hepatitis B or C) than a toxic release that killed thousands. Yet the extent of the harm caused by the biohazardous materials might not be immediately apparent, and if the number of cases of infected people gradually increased, fear and panic could spread among the populace. The impact of the weapon using medical waste would still not approach that of the toxic release. Nonetheless, the uncertainty surrounding the biohazardous weapon's effect could serve to enhance that effect and produce a significant result given the materials used.

In the next chapter, we will look at some examples of how toxic weapons have been used by both state and nonstate actors.

Chapter Three

RECENT USE OF AND THINKING ABOUT TOXIC WEAPONS

As discussed in the previous chapters, toxic weapons offer a number of advantages to state and nonstate actors who seek to advance their military and political objectives. Industrial chemicals and chemical waste are both plentiful, providing a low-cost and easily assembled option that can be deployed through a variety of means—including air delivery (missiles and rockets), land delivery (cars, trucks, or containers in legal or illegal transit or at a stationary location), or sea delivery (barges and small craft). Toxic weapons can cause physical harm to humans and can damage and contaminate infrastructure. They can also create temporary panic or chaos, thereby exerting an asymmetrical effect on information and psychological operations (IO/PSYOP). The advantages of toxic weapons are offset somewhat by the uncertainty surrounding their effects; these weapons are often difficult to target, and their physical impacts can be inconsistent. Such uncertainties, however, can make them the weapons of choice for insurgents, terrorists, and rogue nations looking mostly for tactical and/or psychological advantage.

This chapter provides an overview of recent incidents involving toxic weapon use, focusing on two especially prominent types of toxic warfare: poisonings and the use of chemicals and smoke. It ends with a discussion of notable developments in toxic warfare, including the use of toxic weapons within more sophisticated terrorist networks; a growing opportunism concerning the materials used to make toxic weapons; and an apparent increase in interest in using such weapons.

A caveat to the reader is in order, however. The goal of this chapter is to offer a relatively broad view of the range of possibilities associated with toxic weapons. This discussion is meant as a qualitative overview and does not purport to offer a quantitative analysis of the risks associated with particular kinds of toxic weapons or the consequences of specific attacks. It is hoped that the current discussion can help identify areas requiring further quantitative analysis.

POISONING WITH CHEMICALS, SEWAGE, AND PESTICIDES

Many recent incidents of toxic warfare have involved poisoning with chemicals, sewage, or pesticides. All these substances can be used to interfere with military operations, disrupt the functioning of civilian infrastructure, cause physical harm, and instill fear among the general populace.[1]

Episodes of poisoning have a long history in toxic warfare. In 1986, the Liberation Tigers of Tamil Eelam (LTTE) poisoned tea with potassium cyanide in an effort to cripple the Sri Lankan tea export industry.[2] In December 1989, during civil unrest in Romania in conjunction with the collapse of the Ceaucescu government, the water supply for the city of Sibiu was poisoned with an organophosphate by Romanian nationalists.[3] In March 1992, water tanks at a

---

[1]Water poisonings can occur, but only under the right conditions. Chlorine residuals and actual consumption of water nowadays limit toxic effectiveness and the utility of the fluoroacetates. According to Siegfried Franke, in terms of poisonings, some substances work well in waterworks, food supplies, and crops. The prerequisite for these applications is great resistance to hydrolysis or to the formation of equally poisonous products of hydrolysis. Sarin dissolves in water to an unlimited extent and hydrolyzes very slowly, and the same is true of the organic compounds of fluorine, which have been suggested for sabotage and diversion work. Other poisons or chemical warfare agents dissolve in water only to a limited extent, but their solubility and resistance to hydrolysis suffice to achieve effective contaminations. See Siegfried Franke, *Manual of Military Chemistry*, Vol. 1., Berlin: Deutscher Militärverlag, 1967, pp. 30 and 139. See also William H. Monday, *Thinking the Unthinkable: Attacking Fresh Water Supplies*, master's thesis, Naval Postgraduate School, Monterey, CA, AD-B241, December 1998.

[2]See Abraham D. Sofaer, George D. Wilson, and Sidney D. Dell, *The New Terror: Facing the Threat of Biological and Chemical Weapons*, Stanford, CA: Hoover Institution, 1999, p. 82.

[3]See "A History of Biological and Chemical Threats to Water Supply," *International Defense Review*, Vol. 32, No. 1, January 1, 1999, p. 58.

Turkish army base outside Istanbul were poisoned with potassium cyanide; suspicion was aroused when two empty 25-kg boxes were found next to the water tanks and a layer of foam was seen on the water. An investigation concluded that the Kurdish Workers Party (PKK) had launched the attack.[4] In 1994, during heavy fighting on the Thai-Cambodian border near Pailin, more than a dozen Khmer Royal Armed Forces combatants died after having consumed water from streams and ponds poisoned by opposing Khmer Rouge forces.[5] In 2000, Chechen rebels attempted to poison Russian soldiers with an unidentified toxic substance found in wine delivered to the soldiers by Chechen civilians.[6]

The Israeli-Palestinian Conflict

The Israeli-Palestinian conflict has involved the use of pesticides, other chemicals, and sewage in toxic weapons. In October 1997, Israeli counterterrorism official Meir Dagan stated that he was afraid that toxic weapons were about to be used in the Israeli-Palestinian conflict.[7] During the same month, Israeli settlers from Gosh Etzion sprayed a chemical on Arab grape farms in the Ertas and Khader villages south of Bethlehem, ruining hundreds of grapevines and as many as 17,000 metric tons of grapes.[8] On June 19, 1999, Hamas announced plans to poison water supplies is Israel with "chemical sub-

---

[4]The amount in question would not have caused death. See "Turks Report Attempt to Poison Air Force Unit," Reuters, March 28, 1992, as quoted in Monday, *Thinking the Unthinkable*, December 1998, p. 137.

[5]See "A History of Biological and Chemical Threats to Water Supply," January 1, 1999. Although the number of deaths caused by poisoning was much smaller than that caused by land mines in the region, the use of poison was nonetheless an effective terror weapon.

[6]See Jason Pate, Gary Ackerman, and Kimberly McCloud, *2000 WMD Terrorism Chronology: Incidents Involving Sub-National Actors and Chemical, Biological, Radiological, or Nuclear Materials*, Monterey, CA: Center for Nonproliferation Studies, available at http://cns.miis.edu/pubs/reports/cbrn2k.htm.

[7]See Yigal Sarna and Anat Tal-Shir, "Most of All He Likes to Disguise Himself and Operate in Enemy Territory," *Yediot Aharonot*, October 24, 1997, pp. 16–19, accessed from FBIS-FTS-19971102000227.

[8]See Shabatai Zvi, "Israeli Settlers Destroy 17,000 Tons of Grapes," *Al-Ayyam*, October 23, 1997, available at http://www.hebron.com/article04-10-23-97.html.

stances."[9] In November 1999, Israeli forces arrested an unidentified Hamas leader who had charts, tables, and specific instructions for mixing toxic substances into usable weapons. The materials were all obtained locally and were easy to disguise.[10]

In 2000, both Hezbollah and Hamas used insecticide in rockets or threatened to burn Israeli factories where industrial wastes were stored, creating clouds of toxic vapors.[11] In February 2000, Turkish authorities seized eight units of an unknown toxic substance during a weapons raid of Hezbollah facilities in Gazientep.[12] In June 2000, Palestinian news sources reported that Israeli settlers from the Efrat settlement on the West Bank had deliberately released sewer water into agricultural fields maintained by Palestinian settlers in the village of Khadder, near Bethlehem. According to local farmers, the release of the wastewater was part of an "annual tradition" designed to force Palestinian farmers off of their land.[13] In September 2001, Israelis used chemical fertilizer in a mass poisoning of 145 sheep and goats in the West Bank.[14]

Pesticides or other chemicals are also suspected to have been used as part of an attack by Palestinian suicide bombers in December 2001. Hazardous materials were found in a device detonated by the attackers, creating what officials believed was a crude attempt to make a

---

[9]See Gavin Cameron, Jason Pate, Diana McCauley, and Lindsay DeFazio, *1999 WMD Terrorism Chronology: Incidents Involving Sub-National Actors and Chemical, Biological, Radiological, and Nuclear Materials*, Monterey, CA: Center for Nonproliferation Studies, Vol. 7, No. 2, Summer 2000, available at http://cns.miis.edu/pubs/npr/vol07/72/wmdchr72.htm.

[10]"Hot Mish'al," Channel 2 Television Network, November 8, 1999, accessed from FBIS-FTS-19991109000932.

[11]See Paul Bedard, "Danger Zone," *U.S. News & World Report*, March 6, 2000, p. 10.

[12]See Pate, et al., *2000 WMD Terrorism Chronology*.

[13]See "Settlers Pump Sewerage Water into Palestinian Groves," Palestine Information Network, June 21, 2000, available at http://www.palestine-info.net/daily_news/prev_editions/2000/June2000/21June.htm#9.

[14]See Tracy Wilkinson, "Microcosm of the Mideast Conflict in a Dead Flock," *Los Angeles Times*, September 1, 2001, p. A3; and Stefan H. Leader, "The Rise of Terrorism," *Security Management*, April 2001. The conclusion was reached after investigators found a large amount of cyanide along with manuals in the bombers' residences.

chemical weapon. One of the bombs used in the attacks on Jerusalem appears to have been immersed in some kind of chemical. An Israeli official noted that Palestinian bombers had apparently experimented with their explosive devices in order to "maximize the effect" by spreading hazardous materials in the vicinity of the blast.

CHEMICALS, GASES, AND SMOKE

Chemicals, gases, and smoke can be used as part of traditional weaponry such as bombs and rockets or as weapons in themselves— as, for example, when industrial facilities are attacked to cause a chemical release. Several such uses are examined in this section.

Bosnia

In the first week of August 1993, Bosnian Muslim forces used chlorine in 120mm shells on three occasions against Bosnian Serb forces. A few shells were fired at each decisive point of the battle either to facilitate a Muslim breakthrough or to stall the Serbs' advance. United Nations Protection Force (UNPROFOR) observers described the weapons as "crude, almost like home-made stuff with a radius of only 20 meters." The order to use chlorine for defense purposes came from Andjelko Makar, Chief of Staff of the Second Corps of the Bosnia-Herzegovina Army based in Tuzla.[15]

Croatia

Serbian forces have frequently used toxic weapons, both as traditional weapons and through attacks on industrial facilities. As described in the introduction to this report, Serbian forces in Croatia used rockets, bombs, artillery, machine gun tracers, and mortars on six occasions between 1993 and 1995 to attack the Petrochemia plant, which produced fertilizer, carbon black, and light-fraction petroleum products. Hazardous substances at the plant included ammonia; sulfur (which poses a hydrogen sulfide inhalation hazard

---

[15]See Yossef Bodansky, "Bosnian Muslim Forces' First Combat Use of Chemical Weapons," *Defense and Foreign Affairs Strategic Policy*, August 31, 1993, p. 16.

in the event of a fire); nitric, sulfuric, and phosphoric acids; heavy oil; and formaldehyde.[16]

Other chemical plants were attacked in the Croatian war. Serbian forces used rockets containing cluster bombs on a natural gas refinery in eastern Slavonia where ethane, propane, and butane were stored. Serbian forces also struck a chemical plant near the town of Jovan, releasing 72 tons of anhydrous ammonia and forcing the evacuation of 32,000 residents. Mortar attacks were launched on the Herbos pesticide plant located in Croatia's industrial center at Sisak. In addition, Serbian forces attacked large fuel storage tanks along the highway from Belgrade to the outskirts of Zagreb and started large fires at Osijek, Sisak, and Karlovak.[17] The refinery at Sisak, which produced liquefied petroleum gas (LPG), fuels, petroleum coke, and solvents, was hit particularly hard. Thousands of Serbian artillery rounds hit 38 storage tanks, destroying all of them. U.S. modeling efforts indicate that had the attacks destroyed existing stored chemical containers, lethal concentrations of chemicals would have covered a wide area.

Toxic warfare was also used against the Serbs. Muslim forces in Tuzla threatened chemical use in order to hold off a Serbian attack against the city, vowing to release large quantities of chlorine gas from railroad tank cars if the city was assaulted—despite the large number of friendly casualties that would have resulted from such an action.[18]

Sri Lanka

During the 1990s, the LTTE used chemical waste to attack industrial facilities on several occasions as a means of creating confusion at strategic points. In November 1995, LTTE forces launched a gas attack on Sri Lankan troops in a bid to lift a siege on the rebel bastion of Jaffna, sparking heavy battles that left 84 dead on both sides. The

---

[16]See FM 90-10-1, Q-8–Q-9. Refineries are usually designed so that two fires can be controlled and suppressed at one time, but at this refinery firefighters had to fight as many as five major fires simultaneously.

[17]Ibid.

[18]Ibid.

toxic attack was the first since 1990, when the LTTE fired chlorine gas cylinders into a besieged military camp near Batticaloa on the east coast.[19]   In 2001, Tamil rebels attacked the Bandaranaike International Airport and military base with mortars. The first wave of attacks, launched at 3:30 a.m., targeted industrial and fuel facilities at the airport to create a fire and smoke diversion, while a second wave of mortars was aimed at both commercial and military aircraft. The resulting damage claimed 12 aircraft, costing millions of dollars, and closed the airport for a day.[20]

Chechnya and Russia

In Chechnya, both Chechens and Russians have accused each other of ammonia and chlorine attacks. In 1995, a Chechen soldier described a Russian weapon that released an unknown toxic chemical:

> But one day an aircraft appeared and dropped a strange bomb. That is, it fell very strangely, rather slowly, flipping over and over the whole time. It detonated at a height of 120 meters above the ground and lots and lots of these little petals came out. They came whirling slowly down. At first we thought they were mines you know, the kind you scatter and if you step on them they blow off your foot. But then, after a while, they began to explode spontaneously. Not very loudly, but there were bangs throughout the forest. I went up and picked up one of these things. It went off in my hand. In the middle, between two petals, was a kind of capsule, about as big as a vial of brilliant green antiseptic. Some sort of liquid splashed out onto my clothing and a bit landed on my hand. I threw my jacket out, but later on there was a burning sensation on my hand, although I had immediately washed off the liquid with water. The smell was so bad it was impossible to breathe. It was disgusting. And there seemed to be a bit of a

---

[19]See Agence France-Presse, November 25, 1995, accessed from FBIS-FTS-19951125000450.

[20]See "Tamil Rebels Raid Sri Lankan Airport," *Washington Post*, July 25, 2001, p. 14.

> smell of garlic. Then, a couple of days later, the leaves began to fall from the trees.[21]

This incident is particularly interesting because of the delivery system used, which was similar to a fuel-air explosive. However, the weapon was used to deliver not a mainstream chemical agent but some type of toxic substance or waste. Clearly, the Russians were modifying existing weaponry.[22] The incident also suggests something of the psychological uncertainty surrounding toxic warfare. The soldier recognizes that something toxic has landed on his clothing but doesn't know what it is. He also reports a feeling of revulsion at the substance's odor and has difficulty breathing as a result.

In both 1999 and 2000, Chechen rebels launched toxic attacks involving chemical and petroleum waste. On December 10, 1999, Chechens detonated previously prepared containers of chlorine and ammonia. As part of a battle with federal forces, they also ignited five oil wells, which burned up to 200 tons of oil per day.[23] The resulting smoke degraded the Russians' ability to observe the Chechens' actions and hence their ability to conduct military operations. In January 2000, Chechen forces tried to slow a federal force's offensive by blowing up 60-ton-capacity barrels in 111 rail cars loaded with chlorine solution and petroleum and emitting clouds of toxic gases.[24]

---

[21]See Alexander Mnatsakanyan, "Were Chemical Weapons Used in Chechnya?" *Izvestia*, August 24, 1995, pp. 1–2, accessed from FBIS-FTS-19970502001427.

[22]Based on interviews with Eric Croddy from the Monterey Institute of International Studies and with analysts at the Armed Forces Medical Intelligence Center (AFMIC), July 2001.

[23]See "Grozny Gas Cloud Blown in Wrong Direction," Russian Public Television First Channel Network, December 29, 1999, accessed from FBIS-FTS-19991229001437; and "Five Oil Wells Still Ablaze in Chechnya," RIA, November 30, 1999, accessed from FBIS-FTS-19991201000318.

[24]See "Toxic Cloud in Chechnya: Rebels Detonate Chlorine Tank," RIA, December 10, 1999, accessed from FBIS-FTS-1999121000813; Pate et al., *2000 WMD Terrorism Chronology*; Mikhail Supotnitskii, "The Second Coming of Chlorine," *Nezavisimoye voyennoe obozrenie*, No. 1, January 2000, p. 4, accessed from FBIS-CEP-20000127000079; and Yevgenii V. Antonov, "Threat of Terrorist Attack Using Weapons of Mass Destruction from Chechnya," *Yadernyy kontrol*, No. 2, March–April 2001, pp. 55–70, accessed from FBIS-CEP-20010610000001.

Russia began to take the toxic threat seriously by sending NBC troops to the area and issuing gas masks and other protective measures for soldiers.[25] Military intelligence reported that mines, barrels, cisterns, and canisters filled with chlorine, ammonia, liquid nitrogen, and low-level radioactive waste stolen from medical and research waste disposal facilities[26] near Grozny had been placed at the intersections of major streets.[27] It is not entirely clear what Chechen rebels hoped to achieve through this particular combination of chemicals. In March 2000, Russian raids on Chechen positions in Grozny found ten tons of chlorine in preparation for deployment.[28]

Another example of the psychological impact of toxic weapons occurred in 2001, when rumors spread throughout Russia and the Persian Gulf of a Chechen plan to use chemicals. A Chechen chemist by the name of "Chitigov" (who was linked to the Chechen Arab warlord Khattab), together with "renowned chemist al-Khazur" from the United Arab Emirates, was reported to be trying to invent a chemical bomb in field conditions. The bomb was to be constructed from materials easily obtained from glass factories.[29] Rumors such

---

[25]See Andrei Korbut, "Chechnya: The Ecological Threat Is Growing," *Nezavisimoye voyennoye obozrenie*, No. 176, January 28, 2000, available at http://nvo.ng.ru/wars/2000-01-28/2_ecohazard.html. See also Olga Oliker, *Russia's Chechen Wars 1994–2000: Lessons from Urban Combat*, MR-1289-A, Santa Monica: RAND, 2001.

[26]Medical waste as a potential toxic weapon also needs to be defined more clearly. In terms of biological sources, thousands of hospitals around the world produce millions of tons of infectious and medical waste every day. Clinics, colleges and universities, diagnostic laboratories, pharmaceutical companies, mortuary facilities, and doctors' offices also generate waste. Biological toxins can include human blood and blood products, cultures and stocks of infectious agents, pathological wastes, contaminated wastes from patient care, discarded biological materials, contaminated animal carcasses, body parts, bedding, and contaminated equipment. In addition, the disposal of infectious and medical waste is a problem because of its potential to transmit disease. Because commercial services for infectious and medical waste disposal are either poor or nonexistent in most areas of the world, these wastes may constitute a serious health hazard for military forces. The primary hazard is that these wastes remain infectious for years if left untreated.

[27]See Korbut, "Chechnya: The Ecological Threat Is Growing," January 28, 2000. See also Oliker, *Russia's Chechen Wars 1994–2000*, 2001.

[28]See "Snipers, Small Rebel Groups Remain in Grozny," ITAR-TASS, March 12, 2000, accessed from FBIS-CEP-20000312000074.

[29]See Timofey Borisov, "Smear a Grenade with Glue and Rain Down Hell," *Rossiyskaya gazeta*, August 30, 2001, as cited in "Paper Profiles Chechen Manufacturer

as this suggest the potential psychological impact of toxic weapons, which are made to seem more powerful than they really are. In the past, Chechens have used information operations to exaggerate their chemical and biological weapon (CBW) capabilities.

TRENDS IN TOXIC WARFARE: ESCALATION OF USE, INCREASED SOPHISTICATION, EXOTIC COMBINATIONS

Al-Qaeda and Osama bin Laden

The experience of Al-Qaeda and Osama bin Laden points to the dangerous combination of easy-to-obtain toxic weaponry and sophisticated terrorist networks. Toxic weapons seem to be used to an increasing extent in conjunction with more complex forms of organization, training, and equipment. Ever since the 1993 World Trade Center car bombings, when Al-Qaeda used cyanide in a bungled attempt to cause a toxic attack as well, Al-Qaeda has shown an interest in toxic warfare.[30] Al-Qaeda has experimented with cyanide gas in Derunta, Afghanistan.[31] Another bin Laden cell in Africa planned a cyanide attack in Europe.[32] After the September 11 terrorist attacks on the United States, U.S. Attorney General John Ashcroft told the Senate Judiciary Committee that several individuals linked to the hijackers had fraudulently obtained or attempted to obtain hazardous material transportation licenses.[33] While Al-Qaeda has a number of options available to it, toxic warfare may certainly be one of them.

---

of Toxic Weapons," accessed from FBIS-CEP-20010830000180. The same recipes are found in Osama bin Laden's training manual.

[30]See Craig Pyes and William C. Rempel, "Poison Gas Plot Alleged in Europe," *Los Angeles Times*, November 12, 2001, p. 10.

[31]See James Risen and Judith Miller, "Al Qaeda Sites Show Skills in Chemicals," *New York Times*, November 11, 2001, p. B1. See also Rory McCarthy, "Inside Bin Laden's Chemical Bunker," *The Guardian*, November 17, 2001; Keith B. Richburg, "Bin Laden and Bombs," *Washington Post*, November 22, 2001, p. A1; and Tom Walker, "Al-Qaeda's Secrets: Bin Laden's Camps Reveal Chemical Weapon Ambition," *Sunday Times* (UK), November 25, 2001.

[32]See Pyes and Rempel, "Poison Gas Plot Alleged in Europe," November 12, 2001, pp. 1 and 10.

[33]See "FBI Starts Nationwide Records Check on HAZMAT Truckers," CNN Online, September 26, 2001, available at http://www.cnn.com.

The ELN and FARC

While the combination of toxic warfare with increasingly sophisticated terrorist networks represents one trend, increased opportunism in the use or combination of toxic substances represents another. In March 1998, for example, the ELN (the Army of National Liberation) mortar attacks outside Cucuta, Colombia, included two explosive charges at a checkpoint, killing Colombian soldier Alberto Moreno Vesga. According to a medical report, the ELN used "fecal material in the explosive devices, causing a high level of contamination in the wounds. Soldier Moreno died from wounds suffered on the arms, [and] legs, and a severe [sepsis] as a result of the fecal substances placed in the aforementioned explosives." A stream of toxic attacks has subsequently occurred. In late 2000, the ELN attacked the police department in Cajibio with sulfuric acid and ammonia. In March 2001, FARC (the Revolutionary Armed Forces of Colombia) attacked the police station in Puerto Lieras with pipe bombs that were loaded with glue, sulfuric acid, gasoline, tar, and feces.[34] In September 2001, FARC attacked the Huila police department with unidentified pulmonary agents thought to be chlorine.

LTTE Sea and Land Attacks

The Tamil Sea Tigers (LTTE)[35] have used smoke and vapors both to create casualties and to cause deception, sometimes through elaborately staged or sophisticated means. In September 2001, the Tamil Sea Tigers attacked Bandaranaike Airport, destroying half of the Sri Lankan air fleet and causing millions of dollars of damage. Included was an attack on the airport's fuel depot that was aimed at spreading smoke and vapors.[36] The attack was intended to produce—and indeed resulted in—a spectacular mess that destroyed the fuel depot while also causing confusion and eventual military operations. One month later, in October 2001, a suicide squad from the LTTE sea

---

[34]See "FARC Allegedly Using Acid, Tar, Feces to Make Bombs," *El Tiempo*, September 6, 2001, accessed from FBIS-LAP-20010906000034.

[35]The Tamil Sea Tigers is the oceangoing version of the Tamil Tigers.

[36]See Rohan Gunaratna, "Intelligence Failures Exposed by Tamil Tigers Airport Attack," *Jane's Intelligence Review*, September 2001, pp. 14–17.

forces attacked the MV Silk Pride at sundown as the ship approached the Haffna peninsula. The oil tanker, carrying 225 tons of low-sulfur diesel, 160 tones of kerosene oil, and 275 tons of auto diesel, caught on fire.[37] LTTE fighters later participated in yet another toxic attack in an effort to interrupt Sri Lanka's economy.[38]

RAISING THE LEVEL OF VIOLENCE?

This review of incidents involving toxic warfare suggests that interest in the use of such weapons may well be on the rise. Recent raids on Al-Qaeda cells both in Europe and in Afghanistan have uncovered manuals clearly illustrating that Al-Qaeda terrorists were thinking, among other things, about deploying toxic weapons. Those who use toxic weapons are also taking whatever opportunities become available to bend the definition of chemical warfare and conventional conflict through their choice of toxic materials and tactics. By breaking down the barriers concerning the types of materials that are used in attacks, terrorists and insurgents are looking to increase their opportunities to catch the adversary off guard and create uncertainty. These asymmetrical warfare options are by design far from those described by chemical warfare treaties and international warfare regulations. Terrorists are also incorporating toxic weapons into more complex preparation and planning strategies.

Taken together, these developments suggest that nonstate actors may be attempting to increase their military prowess through the use of toxic weapons. What this could mean for the United States and the U.S. Air Force will be the subject of the next two chapters.

---

[37]See "Further on Tamil Tigers Attacking Oil Tanker in Sri Lanka," Agence France-Presse, October 30, 2001, accessed from FBIS-SAP-20011030000111.

[38]See "Guerrilla Suicide Boat Hits Sri Lankan Oil Tanker," Reuters, October 30, 2001.

Chapter Four

TOXIC THREATS IN EXPEDITIONARY SETTINGS

U.S. forces have faced the specter of toxic attacks for some time. Typically, these attacks have been considered within the context of operations against countries such as North Korea and the former Soviet Union, and the primary weapons of concern have been militarized chemical and biological agents. However, the United States has given scant consideration to the use of more expedient toxic agents or to the damage that something short of chemical and biological warfare agents could cause.

Although U.S. operations have not yet faced repeated threats from toxic weapons,[1] that possibility clearly exists, particularly in light of the wide availability of toxic materials. Water supplies in areas of operations are vulnerable to intentional and accidental contamination. Toxic waste poses yet another threat, especially because an increasing number of U.S. operations are being conducted in urban industrial areas with decaying and wrecked chemical infrastructures.

U.S. forces frequently operate in environments in which there are toxic materials, particularly industrial chemicals. A number of these chemicals have the potential to interfere with U.S. operations in a significant manner across the range of military operations. Most toxic weapons can be released as vapors—which, as noted earlier, tend to remain concentrated downwind from the release point, in

---

[1]Previous studies of airfield intrusions and attacks show that quick attacks were the most successful. See David A. Shlapak and Alan Vick, "*Check Six Begins on the Ground*": *Responding to the Evolving Ground Threat to U.S. Air Force Bases*, MR-606-AF, Santa Monica: RAND, 1995; and Alan Vick, *Snakes in the Eagle's Nest: A History of Ground Attacks on Air Bases*, MR-553-AF, Santa Monica: RAND, 1995.

natural low-lying areas such as valleys, ravines, or man-made structures; or in any area with low air circulation. Explosions can create and spread liquid hazards, and vapors may condense to liquids in cold air.[2]

The U.S. military is currently seeking to improve its capabilities in responding to a range of possible terrorist threats, and toxic warfare is one such threat. Many U.S. military field manuals and related documents are in the process of being updated, and organizing, training, and equipping for toxic warfare are among the issues being addressed.[3]

This chapter focuses on risk and planning issues for U.S. forces engaged in expeditionary settings. We first examine the risks from toxic warfare for such operations. We then look at the current state of knowledge regarding such threats and identify gaps that need to be filled.

U.S. OPERATIONS AND TOXIC WARFARE IN THE 1990S

Although the United States has had limited experience with toxic warfare, a review of past incidents involving toxic threats can point to some areas of potential vulnerability. One threat arises from toxic smoke in the field of operations.

The threat from toxic smoke is greatest for ground forces deployed to unstable areas, which today include Afghanistan, Pakistan, Uzbekistan, and Kyrgyzstan. Operation Desert Storm provides an example of the confusion and damage that can result from toxic

---

[2]Four industry-standard dispersion models measure the spread of toxic materials: AFTOX, DEGADIS, INPUFF, and SLAB. See Breeze Software and Services, *Breeze Haz Materials,* available at http://www.breeze-software.com/content/haz/.

[3]The Chemical Corps Doctrine and Development Division of the U.S. Army Chemical School (USACMLS) conducted a study on lapses in doctrine regarding toxic warfare. They deemed that JP 1.02 (Joint Warfare of the Armed Forces of the United States), FM 101-5-1 (Operational Terms and Graphics), FM 3-100 (Chemical Operations Principles and Fundamentals), FM 3-3 (Chemical and Biological Contamination Avoidance), FM 3-11 (Flame, Riot Control Agents and Herbicide Operations), FM 3-18 (Special NBC Reconnaissance), and FM 34-54 (Battlefield Technical Intelligence) all need to be rewritten. See *USACMLS Doctrine Changes,* available at http://www.wood.army.mil/cmdoc/doctrine%20changes.pdf.

smoke, which can be used to impair vision and disrupt military operations. From January 25 to 27, 1991, Iraqi troops created a massive oil spill off Kuwait that ignited more than 700 Kuwaiti oil fields, sending smoke throughout the area of operations. In response, U.S. F-111Fs launched GBU-15 guided bombs that managed to destroy oil manifolds connecting storage tanks to the terminal. While this action drastically cut the flow of oil, oil fires continued to release large quantities of poisonous gases. In addition, some wells failed to ignite, forming vast pools of raw crude that covered hundreds of acres and created potential firetraps. So great was the smoke from burning oil wells that visibility was severely limited for coalition air forces in the Kuwaiti theater of operations (KTO). For fliers, the smoke created abrupt and repeated transitions from clear skies to instrument flying conditions. The weather also added to the problem, with black-spattering, oil-laden rain clogging engines in the air and on the ground.[4]

U.S. armed forces are also subject to contaminated supplies. Contamination can result from poor security on the part of outside suppliers as well as from the presence of toxic waste in and around the area of operations. One example of the risk of water contamination arose during Operation Just Cause. When U.S. forces landed in Somalia, the first priority for allied commanders was to supply fresh water to their forces on the ground. A plant located in Saudi Arabia had initially been commissioned to deliver thousands of pallets of bottled water at a cost of millions of dollars. Upon their delivery to Somalia, however, some of the bottles were found by U.S. Army chemists to be contaminated with fecal matter, and the entire lot was dumped. Until alternative sources of water could be found, most

---

[4]See Federation of American Scientists, *Reaching Globally, Reaching Powerfully: The United States Air Force in the Gulf War—A Report—September 1991*, available at http://www.fas.org/man/dod-101/ops/docs/desstorm.htm; Federation of American Scientists, *Chapter VI—The Air Campaign*, available at http://www.fas.org/irp/imint/docs/cpgw6/cpgw_ch6_execute.htm; and U.S. General Accounting Office, *Operation Desert Storm: Evaluation of the Air Campaign*, Washington, D.C., GAO/NSIAD-97-134, June 1997, p. 5, Appendix IV:3. The Armed Forces Medical Intelligence Center stated that the detonation of the oil wells was intended to create flame barriers and to give off hydrogen sulfide gas contained in oil diverted from deep, high-pressure wells. If the petroleum is ignited in the presence of large quantities of natural gas, the effects would be similar to a fuel air explosive (FAE). See Federation of American Scientists, *AFMIC Weekly Wire 48-90*, available at http://www.fas.org/irp/gulf/cia/970129/970110_WW48090_90_0001.html.

U.N. contingents had to make do with Kenyan boxed water that was deemed clean. French forces had water flown in daily from Europe, which needed to be well guarded at French bunkers.[5]

U.S. THINKING ABOUT TOXIC THREATS

Throughout the 1990s, the growing awareness of the threat posed by NBC weapons provided a foundation for learning more about the phenomenon. Toxic weapons using industrial chemicals are relatively easy to produce, as there is no need to synthesize, process, improvise agent delivery devices, or conduct testing. Little or no specialized knowledge of the manufacturing process is required. Toxic substances such as chlorine, phosgene, and hydrogen cyanide can easily be acquired and adapted.[6] For those seeking to use toxic weapons, the biggest threat is to avoid detection by authorities. Yet the wide availability of the substances used to make toxic weapons makes detection difficult.

An example of more formal U.S. thinking about potential toxic threats can be found in the 1997 *Assessment of the Impact of Chemical and Biological Weapons on Joint Operations in 2010*. This study examined, among other threats from chemical warfare, the potential for toxic weapons to disrupt U.S. military operations. The study identified local and asymmetrical attacks as the most likely threats to U.S. forces.[7] More specifically, the report examined a scenario in which a "blue team" uses chemical agents thinly to avoid lethal levels, which allows the force to impede U.S. military operations while complicating detection and cleanup. This report provides an idea of broad U.S. thinking about chemical weapons, al-

---

[5]See Venter, "Poisoned Chalice Poses Problems," January 1, 1999.

[6]See U.S. General Accounting Office, S*tatement of Henry L. Hinton, Jr., Assistant Comptroller General, National Security and International Affairs Division, Testimony Before the Subcommittee on National Security, Veterans Affairs, and International Relations, Committee on Government Reform, House of Representatives, Combating Terrorism: Observations on the Threat of Chemical and Biological Terrorism*, Washington, D.C, GAO/T-NSIAD-00-50, October 20, 1999.

[7]See U.S. General Accounting Office, *Report to Congressional Requesters, Chemical Weapons: DOD Does Not Have a Strategy to Address Low-Level Exposures*, Washington, D.C., GAO/NSIAD-98-228, September 1998.

though it does not offer a separate assessment of the response needed for toxic weapons.

In 1998, the Office of the Secretary of Defense (OSD) assessed the potential for a chemical attack to cause significant delays in the deployment of forces and to impair mission success. Although this OSD report did not specifically address toxic threats to the forces, it did examine the impact of a chemical or biological attack on an installation serving as a power projection site (i.e., one that our forces would use as a launching point in a time of crisis), using Fort Bragg and Pope Air Force Base (both located in Fayetteville, North Carolina) as its focus. The Pope/Bragg study concluded that chemical/biological attacks would significantly delay deploying forces and had the potential to impair the mission achievement of those forces. It further suggested that many of the vulnerabilities observed could be minimized through a preparedness program consisting of planning, training, exercises, and equipment. In consonance with this conclusion, the study recommended that DoD establish a program of installation preparedness to enhance awareness, plans, and preparations for the possibility of chemical or biological attacks at key force projection sites. This need formed the basis of the Pope/Bragg pilot.[8]

The U.S. Army Soldier and Biological Chemical Command (SBCCOM) has also developed a preparedness program for addressing issues relating to WMD. This program, which is directed toward U.S. military installations and has been successfully piloted at Fort Bragg and Pope Air Force Base, is based on the Army's experience in the Nunn-Lugar-Domenici Domestic Preparedness Program and on its participation in the Pope/Bragg study. The program's objective was to validate an approach toward preparing key military installations to respond to asymmetrical attacks involving WMD. Accordingly, it consisted of planning, training, exercises, and other technical assistance. The program targeted installation commanders and their staffs, installation emergency responders (fire, HAZMAT, and law enforcement/security personnel as well as health care

---

[8]See Paul Wolfowitz, Deputy Secretary of Defense, letter to the Honorable Bob Stump, Chairman, Committee on Armed Services, U.S. House of Representatives, Washington, D.C., April 25, 2001.

providers), and their counterparts in the local, state, federal, and host-nation communities. [9] The pilot programs succeeded in reducing delays in deployment by 45 percent on average and had a positive impact on the installation's other operations.[10]

Other work remains to be done to ensure that military doctrine adequately addresses the issue of toxic warfare. In conjunction with SBCCOM preparations, the Chemical Corps Doctrine and Development Division of the U.S. Army Chemical School found that several field manuals—JP 1.02, FM 101-5-1, FM 3-100, FM 3-3, FM 3-11, FM 3-18, and FM 34-54—need to be rewritten to reflect the potential for toxic warfare. The school argued that doctrine should be based on the description found in the *Assessment of the Impact of Chemical and Biological Weapons on Joint Operations in 2010*. Combined with the evidence that nonstate actors had been increasingly thinking about toxic warfare, FM 3-100 now pinpoints the need to identify toxic waste sites. [11]

REMAINING ISSUES FOR EXPEDITIONARY OPERATIONS

The level of threat represented by toxic weapons remains to be determined. Should toxic warfare be considered a nuisance or a threat of strategic concern? Although it is impossible to know how extensively toxic weapons will be used in the future, the experience of toxic warfare to date and the kinds of urban operations in which the United States will likely be involved suggest that toxic warfare merits serious consideration as part of future planning strategies. There are several reasons for this conclusion:

- **The United States is not immediately aware of the location of toxic threats.** Overall, the U.S. military is actively aware of the potential for toxic threats, but the identification of specific threats is a painstaking process. In future operations, it is possible that an entire area of operations could be contaminated

---

[9]Ibid.

[10]Ibid.

[11]Ibid. Discussions with AFMIC analysts, 2000–2001.

with toxic waste.[12] Therefore, as the war on terrorism continues, U.S. forces will need to improve their knowledge of the locations of both legal and illegal sources of toxic waste as part of their intelligence assessments and contingencies.[13]

- **At the operational level, U.S. forces currently have no tailored response to toxic warfare in doctrine.** As the U.S. military develops a response to toxic warfare, it will need to provide a doctrinal response to resolve the trade-off between force protection and mobility/agility. One response to the potential for toxic warfare could be to bring chemical kits, protective clothing, cleanup materials, and the like, on every operation. Doing so, however, would impede the mobility and agility of the forces.

  Emergency response exercises and training should also be expanded to incorporate all the elements that could be involved in responding to a toxic attack. Air Force first responders currently exercise with their civilian counterparts on an annual basis, using the Disaster Response Force infrastructure to vary the types of NBC attack to include nuclear/radiological, biological, chemical, incendiary, and explosive materials.[14] The Air Force is investigating the possible use of the SBCCOM Program and services provided by the University of Texas A&M Emergency Responder Training Program. Three interactive training CD-ROMs for the emergency response to terrorism have been published by Headquarters, Air Force Civil Engineer Support Agency (HQ AFCESA) and distributed to all Air Force installations. [15]

- **The use of toxic weapons has implications for U.S. military lift and logistics.** As base security becomes more critical to operations, the vulnerability of key logistics sites has emerged as an

---

[12]Interview with a U.S Navy SEAL, 2001, who asked not to be identified. According to the interviewee, each operation is conducted in failed states filled with toxic waste, sewage, and radioactive waste.

[13]The author participated in the planning process by contributing to classified AFMIC products on toxic warfare and their presence in the Afghan theater.

[14]See Wolfowitz, letter to the Honorable Bob Stump, April 25, 2001.

[15]Ibid.

important issue.[16] Many sites are vulnerable to toxic attack, including ports, airfields, and related fixed sites that serve as choke points. Ports of embarkation (POEs) and en route facilities may be targeted in order to disrupt or inhibit U.S. military deployment both within and outside the threatened theater. For some large-scale operations, the en route structure is limited and may be a particularly lucrative target. Fixed sites are high-value targets for adversary toxic attack. Combat forces are vulnerable both during entry operations and during movement to areas of military operations. Support staging areas as well as rail and road networks are also potential targets, as are intermediate and infrastructure logistics bases. Aerial ports of debarkation (APODs) are vulnerable as well.

The APOD provides an example of how the U.S. Air Force can incorporate the possibility of toxic warfare into its planning. Because each APOD is unique, the size and operational flexibility of any particular site will affect the commander's options for preventing toxic contamination. To minimize the potential for aircraft to be exposed to toxic threats during ground operations, APOD plans need to include expedited offload procedures within the toxic threat area (e.g., engines running, no crew changes or refueling). It must also be recognized that in the event of contamination, some aircraft will not be able to land at or depart from certain areas of an aerial port regardless of its level of toxic preparedness. Instead, contaminated aircraft will need to be thoroughly decontaminated—a rigorous process if high-tech planes with advanced polymers are damaged or destroyed.[17]

• **At the tactical level, U.S. armed forces may not be ready for toxic warfare.** OSD has found a number of problems with preparation for toxic warfare as a subset of an NBC attack. Toxic waste vapors often hug the ground, an issue that is not addressed in some scenarios. On November 15 2001, the Air Force Deputy Chief of Staff/Installations and Logistics issued

---

[16]See David A. Fulghum, "Terrorism Makes Base Protection Critical," *Aviation Week & Space Technology*, June 18, 2001, p. 196.

[17]See U.S. Air Force, *Civil Engineer Emergency Response Operations*, Air Force Manual 32-4004, December 1, 1995, pp. 70–80.

direction and guidance to all Major Commands on installation actions required for preparation of response to terrorist attacks with weapons of mass destruction. The document directed installations to plan, equip, train, and exercise installation emergency reponse capability for terrorist WMD events. Air Force publications to support this policy are in progress.

The Air Force is coordinating several documents to provide needed planning, organization, equipage, training, and exercise/evaluation program policy guidance for commanders and first responders. The planned policy guidance documents implemented Air Force Doctrine Document 2-1.8, *Counter Nuclear, Biological and Chemical Operation*. Other documents include Air Force Policy Directive 10-25, *Full Spectrum Threat Response*; Air Force Instruction 10-2501, *Full Spectrum Threat Response Planning and Operations*; Air Force Handbook 10-2502, *WMD Threat Planning and Response*; and Air Force Instruction 10-2601, *Counter NBC Operations*. The Air Force has developed its Baseline Equipment Data Assessment List in the event of a toxic or NBC attack. [18] Additional training is being developed.

- **Cleanup from a toxic attack may pose a difficult challenge.** Contaminated aircraft pose an especially difficult decontamination challenge, as demonstrated by the oil-laden rain that coalition forces confronted during the Gulf War. Fixed-site decontamination techniques typically focus on fixed facilities and mission support areas such as command, control, communications, computers, and intelligence (C^4I) facilities, supply depots, aerial and sea ports, medical facilities, and maintenance sites. However, cargo may require extensive decontamination measures, specialized and highly sensitive monitoring equipment, and extended weathering or destruction. It is therefore possible that equipment decontamination may have to be delayed until after conflict termination. [19]

In sum, the U.S. military is aware of the threat of toxic warfare, and some progress is being made to raise awareness through U.S. strat-

---

[18] Ibid.

[19] FM 90-10-1, Appendix A.

egy and doctrine. However, more work remains to be done in identifying and locating toxic threats, developing operational and tactical responses to toxic warfare, expanding training for responding to toxic attacks, and devising adequate cleanup procedures. The United States must also address the threat of toxic weapons within the homeland, as will be discussed in the next chapter.

Chapter Five

TOXIC THREATS IN THE UNITED STATES

Toxic warfare is a threat not just for U.S. forces engaged in military operations but also for civilians within the United States. The risk is increased by the wide availability of toxic materials throughout the United States, together with the proximity of industrial operations to urban centers. In fact, the combination of large population centers and multiple toxic material sources poses a range of threats that need not involve warfare; accidents, incompetence, or employee malevolence could all produce a toxic incident with significant implications for civilian populations. Yet the potential for terrorists to use toxic weapons as part of a deliberate attack adds another dimension to this threat.

This chapter focuses on some of the issues relating to toxic threats in the United States and assesses the potential for an effective response in the event of a disaster. It also offers recommendations for civilian-military planning.

AREAS OF VULNERABILITY

U.S. officials have been thinking about toxic warfare attacks on U.S. territory for some time. Prior to the 1996 Atlantic Olympics, for example, federal authorities considered potential threats from improvised chemical devices such as the use of high explosives by terrorists to puncture a train car loaded with chlorine gas. Since 1996, the

United States has routinely taken active measures to prepare for special events.[1]

Awareness has also increased with respect to the potential for toxic attacks involving hazardous materials. Since 1999, the Gilmore Commission has discussed the use of hazardous materials as toxic weapons. Commission members have investigated prevention, preparedness, mitigation, and response for HAZMAT scenarios and incidents in CONUS as well as chemical, biological, radioactive, and nuclear (CBRN), agroterror, and cyber threats.[2]

One issue of great concern remains the potential vulnerability of chemical and industrial facilities within the United States. Although available unclassified sources do not provide sufficient information from which to draw conclusions about the frequency of past attacks that have been planned or executed against industrial facilities, we can get an idea of the potential vulnerability of many such facilities from a recent example involving Greenpeace activists and a Dow Chemical plant near Baton Rouge, Louisiana. In February 2001, Greenpeace activists concerned about security problems in the chemical industry sought to underscore their point by scaling the fence of the plant, and they succeeded in gaining access to the control panel that regulates potentially dangerous discharges into the Mississippi River.[3] The activists' objective was not to release toxic materials into the river but rather to prove that Dow's security procedures were lacking. If terrorists had gained similar access, however, the results could have been devastating. At the plant, industrial chemicals such as chlorine, sulfuric acid, and hydrochloric acid could potentially provide terrorists with the materials necessary to create powerful toxic weapons. A 1999 study by the federal Agency for Toxic Substances and Disease Registry referred to these chemi-

---

[1]See Jonathan Tucker, "National Health and Medical Services Response to Incidents of Chemical and Biological Terrorism" *JAMA*, Vol. 278, August 6, 1997, pp. 362–368, available at http://jama.ama-assn.org/issues/v278n5/ffull/jpp71006.html.

[2]See the materials under the Advisory Panel to Assess Domestic Response Capabilities for Terrorism Involving Weapons of Mass Destruction at http://www.rand.org/nsrd/terrpanel/.

[3]See Eric Pianin, "Toxic Chemicals' Security Worries Officials," *Washington Post*, November 12, 2001, p. A14 .

cals as "effective and readily accessible materials to develop improvised explosives, incendiaries and poisons."[4]

The seriousness of the problem is directly related to the large number of sites in the United States containing chemicals capable of causing harm. Indeed, many of the chemicals used or produced in plants throughout the country have the potential to match or exceed the 1984 disaster in Bhopal, India. This risk is compounded by the frequent movement of these chemicals, typically by rail, through densely populated areas such as Baltimore and Washington.

The toxic threat within the United States is not limited to civilians. An attack could potentially affect or be directed toward one or more of the many military installations located here. Attacks on critical installations or embarkation points could delay, prevent, or degrade U.S. military operations for homeland protection or overseas deployment.

STEPS FOR PROTECTING THE UNITED STATES FROM AND RESPONDING TO TOXIC WARFARE

How well are industrial facilities protected against the possibility of a toxic attack? In the aftermath of September 11, some U.S. industries have increased the precautions taken to protect their facilities. The chemical industry, for example, issued stringent new site security guidelines, and officials say they are in daily contact with the FBI and other federal authorities to prepare for a direct threat against a chemical plant.[5] Protective measures have also been temporarily increased to provide safeguards for industrial facilities and operations as well as to forestall the potential for retaliation during U.S. military operations. For example, immediately after the United States began bombing Afghanistan on October 7, 2001, the U.S. railroad industry imposed a 72-hour moratorium on carrying toxic or dangerous chemicals. These shipments were resumed, however, after the chemical industry argued that chlorine was essential to the continued operation of sewage treatment plants and that there was no evidence such shipments were being targeted by terrorists.

---

[4]Ibid.
[5]Ibid.

The threat from toxic releases remains large. According to "worst-case" scenarios that companies are required by law to file with the Environmental Protection Agency, a single accident at any of the nearly 50 chemical plants operating between Baton Rouge and New Orleans could potentially put at risk 10,000 to one million people.[6] Environmental and hazardous chemical experts say that serious security problems also persist to varying degrees at chemical manufacturing centers in Texas, New Jersey, Delaware, Philadelphia, and Baltimore.[7] The Dow Chemical plant targeted by Greenpeace reported as its potential "worst case" the release of 800,000 pounds of hydrogen chloride, a suffocating gas that would threaten 370,000 people.

At the forefront of toxic warfare in the United States are the first responders—those individuals who are part of any "organization responsible for responding to an incident involving a weapon of mass destruction."[8] First responders include personnel from medical, law enforcement (or security), fire/rescue, HAZMAT, and explosive ordnance disposal (EOD) organizations. First responders receive extensive training and participate in frequent exercises. Yet while such training is likely to provide the basis for an effective initial response to a toxic attack, other crisis response capabilities need to be improved as well.

ISSUES TO BE ADDRESSED

Despite the solid preparedness of first responders, other aspects of the U.S. crisis response network are lacking. Currently, for example, there is no consistent approach toward burden sharing among agencies, particularly with regard to treating casualties. Internet connectivity in many hospitals remains poor, with only 25 percent of laboratories up to federal standards for access and dissemination of information. Moreover, in the event of multiple toxic attacks, the scope of response needed could overwhelm local resources. Most U.S. hospitals are unprepared to deal with the casualties they would

---

[6]This scenario provides an estimate of the radius of a dangerous cloud of escaping gas and how many people could potentially be affected.

[7]See Pianin, "Toxic Chemicals' Security Worries Officials," November 12, 2001.

[8]Defense Authorization Act for FY 2001, in Section 1031.

see in the wake of a terrorist attack with toxic weapons, and hospitals have been slow to train staff and to equip facilities owing to a lack of funds.[9]

Military and civilian crisis response preparedness efforts must also be better coordinated. An opportunity exists for improved synergy between military preparedness and civilian expertise in areas such as HAZMAT. Civilian preparations for toxic threat have increased since September 11, and civilian organizations are improving their knowledge of the nature of the threat and the needed response. Additional organizing, training, and equipping are being provided at the state level. The U.S. military possesses chemical weapon prevention and cleanup expertise that is applicable to homeland security. Civilian organizations and first responders can benefit from working closely with the military in preparing to respond to toxic threats. The military can for its part expand its efforts to coordinate with civilian organizations in the event of a toxic attack. Such information-sharing and coordination efforts will be necessary to preparing an effective response to the threat of toxic weapons, particularly at a time when so many demands are being placed on the resources of civilian and military personnel involved in crisis response.

FINAL THOUGHTS

Toxic warfare has been a reality for some time. Unfortunately, the continued use of small-scale toxic weapons as well as the persistent threat thereof signals that state and nonstate actors alike recognize that they are in possession of a potent new weapon. Foreign adversaries, including both state and insurgent/terrorist interests, increasingly see toxic warfare as a viable weapon for achieving their military and political goals.

U.S. understanding of this threat, while slow to mature, has improved, particularly for current counterterrorism operations. In

---

[9]See Daniel J. DeNoon, "Hospitals Not Ready for Terrorist Attacks," WebMD Medical News, January 26, 2000, available at http://www.webmd.com. Hospitals have three ranked priorities in the event of a HAZMAT incident. The primary duty is to protect current patients, staff, and the facility itself. The secondary duty is to give the best treatment possible to contaminated patients presenting for care. The final concern is to protect the environment outside the facility.

addition, the U.S. military is improving its ability to prevent and respond to toxic warfare. This report has provided a preliminary examination of an increased interest in asymmetrical toxic warfare among state and nonstate actors. U.S. forces—especially the U.S. Air Force—must continue to think about the problem and take appropriate steps for responding to it.

The risks associated with toxic warfare need to be better understood. Planning for military operations and civilian crisis response requires a detailed understanding of the benefits and costs associated with various options for countering toxic weapons. Military personnel and civilian officials are currently planning for a wide range of threats, all of which are competing for a limited pool of resources. While this research has aimed to show that toxic warfare merits greater attention, it has not attempted to quantify the risk by calculating the frequency of toxic attacks in relation to other kinds of risks or by assessing the full consequences of these weapons' use. A quantitative risk assessment should be considered as a means of providing a more thorough evaluation of the problem.

BIBLIOGRAPHY

Agence France-Presse, November 25, 1995, accessed from FBIS-FTS-19951125000450.

"A History of Biological and Chemical Threats to Water Supply," *International Defense Review*, Vol. 32, No. 1, January 1, 1999, p. 58.

Alexander, George A., "Ecoterrorism and Nontraditional Military Threats," *Military Medicine*, Vol. 165, No. 1, January 2000, p. 3.

Antonov, Yevgenii V., "Threat of Terrorist Attack Using Weapons of Mass Destruction from Chechnya," *Yadernyy kontrol*, No. 2, March–April 2001, pp. 55–70, accessed from FBIS-CEP-2001061000001.

Bedard, Paul, "Danger Zone," *U.S. News & World Report*, March 6, 2000, p. 10.

Bodansky, Yossef, "Bosnian Muslim Forces' First Combat Use of Chemical Weapons," *Defense and Foreign Affairs Strategic Policy*, August 31, 1993, p. 16.

Borisov, Timofey, "Smear a Grenade with Glue and Rain Down Hell," *Rossiyskaya gazeta*, August 30, 2001, as cited in "Paper Profiles Chechen Manufacturer of Toxic Weapons," accessed from FBIS-CEP-20010830000180.

Breeze Software and Services, *Breeze Haz Materials*, available at http://www.breeze-software.com/content/haz/.

Cameron, Gavin, Jason Pate, Diana McCauley, and Lindsay DeFazio, *1999 WMD Terrorism Chronology: Incidents Involving Sub-National Actors and Chemical, Biological, Radiological, and Nuclear Materials*, Monterey, CA: Center for Nonproliferation Studies, Vol. 7, No. 2, Summer 2000, available at http://cns.miis.edu/pubs/npr/vol07/72/wmdchr72.htm.

Chemical Warfare: A Burning Issue—Project on Insurgency, Terrorism and Security, available at http://paladin-san-francisco.com/libgas03.htm.

Cockerham, L. G., and B. S. Shane, *Basic Environmental Toxicology*, Boca Raton, FL: CRC Press, 1994.

Dando, Malcolm, "Discriminating Bio-Weapons Could Target Ethnic Groups," *International Defense Review*, Vol. 30, No. 3, March 1, 1997, p. 77.

Dean, John, "Organized Crime Versus the Environment," *Jane's International Police Review*, January 1, 2000, available at Intelink.

DeNoon, Daniel J., "Hospitals Not Ready for Terrorist Attacks," WebMD Medical News, January 26, 2000, available at http://www.webmd.com.

"FARC Allegedly Using Acid, Tar, Feces to Make Bombs," *El Tiempo*, September 6, 2001, accessed from FBIS-LAP-20010906000034.

"FBI Starts Nationwide Records Check on HAZMAT Truckers," CNN Online, September 26, 2001, available at http://www.cnn.com.

Federation of American Scientists, *AFMIC Weekly Wire 48-90* (U), available at http://www.fas.org/irp/gulf/cia/970129/970110_WW48090_90_0001.html.

Federation of American Scientists, *Chapter VI—The Air Campaign*, available at http://www.fas.org/irp/imint/docs/cpgw6/cpgw_ch6_execute.htm.

Federation of American Scientists, *Reaching Globally, Reaching Powerfully: The United States Air Force in the Gulf War—A Report—September 1991*, available at http://www.fas.org/man/dod-101/ops/docs/desstorm.htm.

"Five Oil Wells Still Ablaze in Chechnya," RIA, November 30, 1999, accessed from FBIS-FTS-19991201000318.

"Forced to Take a Lead on Hazardous Materials," *Jane's International Police Review*, January 1, 2000, available at Intelink.

Franke, Siegfried, *Manual of Military Chemistry*, Vol. 1, Berlin: Deutscher Militärverlag, 1967.

Fulghum, David A., "Terrorism Makes Base Protection Critical," *Aviation Week & Space Technology*, June 18, 2001, p. 196.

"Further on Tamil Tigers Attacking Oil Tanker in Sri Lanka," *Agence France-Presse*, October 30, 2001, accessed from FBIS-SAP-20011030000111.

Galeotti, Mark, "Crimes of the New Millennium," *Jane's Intelligence Review*, August 1, 2000, available at Intelink.

Galeotti, Mark, "The New World of Organized Crime," *Jane's Intelligence Review*, September 1, 2000, available at Intelink.

"Grozny Gas Cloud Blown in Wrong Direction," Russian Public Television First Channel Network, December 29, 1999, accessed from FBIS-FTS-19991229001437.

"Guerrilla Suicide Boat Hits Sri Lankan Oil Tanker," Reuters, October 30, 2001.

Gunaratna, Rohan, "Intelligence Failures Exposed by Tamil Tigers Airport Attack," *Jane's Intelligence Review*, September 2001, pp. 14–17.

Hallmark, Brian, et al., *NBC at the NTC: Distraction or Necessity?* internal paper, Santa Monica: RAND, 2002.

Harigel, Gert G., *Chemical and Biological Weapons: Use in Warfare, Impact on Society and Environment*, Carnegie Endowment for International Peace, available at http://www.ceip.org/files/publications/Harigelreport.asp?p=8.

Harigel, Gert G., *The Concept of Weapons of Mass Destruction: Chemical and Biological Weapons, Use in Warfare, Impact on Society and Environment*, presented at the Conference on

Biosecurity and Bioterrorism, Istituto Diplomatico "Mario Toscano," Rome, Italy, September 18–19, 2000.

Hilz, Christoph, *The International Toxic Waste Trade*, New York: Van Nostrand Reinhold, 1992.

"Hot Mish'al," Channel 2 Television Network, November 8, 1999, accessed from FBIS-FTS-19991109000932.

Joha, Ghassan, "Israel's Bid to Dump Toxic Waste in Jordan Foiled," *The Star*, November 30, 2000, accessed from FBIS-IAP-20001130000091.

Joint Doctrine for Operations in Nuclear, Biological, and Chemical (NBC) Environments, Washington, D.C., Joint Publication 3-11, July 11, 2000.

Korbut, Andrei, "Chechnya: The Ecological Threat Is Growing," *Nezavisimoye voyennoye obozrenie*, No. 176, January 28, 2000, available at http://nvo.ng.ru/wars/2000=01=28/2_ecohazard.html.

Leader, Stefan H., "The Rise of Terrorism," *Security Management*, April 1997.

McCarthy, Rory, "Inside Bin Laden's Chemical Bunker," *The Guardian*, November 17, 2001.

Mnatsakanyan, Alexander, "Were Chemical Weapons Used in Chechnya?" *Izvestia*, August 24, 1995, pp. 1–2, accessed from FBIS-FTS-19970502001427.

Monday, William H., *Thinking the Unthinkable: Attacking Fresh Water Supplies*, master's thesis, Naval Postgraduate School, Monterey, CA, AD-B241, December 1998.

Oliker, Olga, *Russia's Chechen Wars 1994–2000: Lessons from Urban Combat*, MR-1289-A, Santa Monica: RAND, 2001.

Overton, E. B., W. D. Sharpe, and P. Roberts, "Toxicity of Petroleum," in L. G. Cockerham and B. S. Shane, *Basic Environmental Toxicology*, Boca Raton, FL: CRC Press, 1994, pp. 133–156.

Pate, Jason, Gary Ackerman, and Kimberly McCloud, *2000 WMD Terrorism Chronology: Incidents Involving Sub-National Actors and Chemical, Biological, Radiological, or Nuclear Materials*, Monterey, CA: Center for Nonproliferation Studies, available at http://cns.miis.edu/pubs/reports/cbrn2k.htm.

Pianin, Eric, "Toxic Chemicals' Security Worries Officials," *Washington Post*, November 12, 2001, p. A14.

Pyes, Craig, and William C. Rempel, "Poison Gas Plot Alleged in Europe," *Los Angeles Times*, November 12, 2001, p. 10.

Reinhardt, P. A., and J. G. Gordon, *Infectious and Medical Waste Management*, Chelsea, MI: Lewis Publishers, 1991.

Richburg, Keith B., "Bin Laden, Bombs and Buddhas; Documents Left in Kabul Detail Foreigners' Roles," *Washington Post*, November 22, 2001, pp. A1, A35.

Risen, James, and Judith Miller, "Al Qaeda Sites Show Skills in Chemicals," *New York Times*, November 11, 2001, p. B1.

Rodier, D. J., and M. G. Zeeman, "Ecological Risk Assessment," in L. G. Cockerham and B. S. Shane, *Basic Environmental Toxicology*, Boca Raton, FL: CRC Press, 1994, pp. 581–604.

Sarna, Yigal, and Anat Tal-Shir, "Most of All He Likes to Disguise Himself and Operate in Enemy Territory," *Yediot Aharonot*, October 24, 1997, pp. 16–19, accessed from FBIS-FTS-19971102000227.

"Settlers Pump Sewerage Water into Palestinian Groves," Palestine Information Network, June 21, 2000, available at http://www.palestine-info.net/daily_news/prev_editions/2000/June2000/21June.htm#9.

Shlapak, David A., and Alan Vick, *"Check Six Begins on the Ground": Responding to the Evolving Ground Threat to U.S. Air Force Bases*, MR-606-AF, Santa Monica: RAND, 1995.

"Snipers, Small Rebel Groups Remain in Grozny," ITAR-TASS, March 12, 2000, accessed from FBIS-CEP-20000312000074.

Sofaer, Abraham D., George D. Wilson, and Sidney D. Dell, *The New Terror: Facing the Threat of Biological and Chemical Weapons*, Stanford, CA: Hoover Institution, 1999.

Soyland, Svend, *Criminal Organizations and Crimes Against the Environment: A Desktop Study*, Turin, Italy: United National Interregional Crime and Justice Research Institute, June 2000.

Spearson, Graham, "Strategic and Security Issues: Forbidden, Not Forgotten," *International Defense Review*, Vol. 30, No. 3, March 1, 1997, available at Intelink.

Supotnitskii, Mikhail, "The Second Coming of Chlorine," *Nezavisimoye voyennoe obozrenie*, No. 1, January 2000, p. 4, accessed from FBIS-CEP-20000127000079.

"Tamil Rebels Raid Sri Lankan Airport," *Washington Post*, July 25, 2001, p. 14.

"Toxic Cloud in Chechnya: Rebels Detonate Chlorine Tank," RIA, December 10, 1999, accessed from FBIS-FTS-1999121000813.

TRANSCOM J5 and AMC officials, personal interviews, July and August 2001.

Tucker, Jonathan, "National Health and Medical Services Response to Incidents of Chemical and Biological Terrorism" *JAMA*, Vol. 278, August 6, 1997, pp. 362–368, available at http://jama.ama-assn.org/issues/v278n5/ffull/jpp71006.html.

Tucker, Jonathan B. (ed.), *Toxic Terror: Assessing Terrorist Use of Chemical and Biological Weapons*, Cambridge, MA: MIT Press, 2000.

"Turks Report Attempt to Poison Air Force Unit, Reuters, March 28, 1992, as quoted in William H. Monday, *Thinking the Unthinkable: Attacking Fresh Water Supplies*, master's thesis, Naval Postgraduate School, Monterey, CA, AD-B241, December 1998, p. 137.

U.S. Air Force, *Civil Engineer Emergency Response Operations*, Air Force Manual 32-4004, December 1, 1995.

U.S. General Accounting Office, *Operation Desert Storm: Evaluation of the Air Campaign*, Washington, D.C., GAO/NSIAD-97-134, June 1997.

U.S. General Accounting Office, *Report to Congressional Requesters, Chemical Weapons: DOD Does Not Have a Strategy to Address Low-Level Exposures*, Washington, D.C., GAO/NSIAD-98-228, September 1998.

U.S. General Accounting Office, *Statement of Henry L. Hinton, Jr., Assistant Comptroller General, National Security and International Affairs Division, Testimony Before the Subcommittee on National Security, Veterans Affairs, and International Relations, Committee on Government Reform, House of Representatives, Combating Terrorism: Observations on the Threat of Chemical and Biological Terrorism*, Washington, D.C., GAO/T-NSIAD-00-50, October 20, 1999.

U.S. General Accounting Office, *Statement of Mark E. Gebicke, Director, Military Operations and Capabilities Issues, National Security and International Affairs Division, Testimony Before the Committee on Veterans' Affairs, U.S. Senate, Chemical and Biological Defense: Observations on DOD's Plans to Protect U.S. Forces*, Washington, D.C., GAO/T-NSIAD-98-83, 1998.

Venter, Al J., "Biological Warfare: The Poor Man's Atomic Bomb," *Jane's Intelligence Review*, Vol. 11, No. 3, March 1, 1999, p. 42.

Venter, Al J., "Poisoned Chalice Poses Problems: The Terrorist Threat to the World's Water," *International Defense Review*, Vol. 32, No. 1, January 1, 1999, p. 57.

Vick, Alan, *Snakes in the Eagle's Nest: A History of Ground Attacks on Air Bases*, MR-553-AF, Santa Monica: RAND, 1995.

Walker, Tom, "Al-Qaeda's Secrets: Bin Laden's Camps Reveal Chemical Weapon Ambition," *Sunday Times* (UK), November 25, 2001.

Wilkinson, Tracy, "Microcosm of the Mideast Conflict in a Dead Flock," *Los Angeles Times*, September 1, 2001, p. A3.

Wolfowitz, Paul, Deputy Secretary of Defense, letter to the Honorable Bob Stump, Chairman, Committee on Armed Services, U.S. House of Representatives, Washington, D.C., April 25, 2001.

Zanders, Jean Pascal, "Assessing the Risk of Chemical and Biological Weapons Proliferation to Terrorists," *Nonproliferation Review*, Fall 1999, pp. 17–34.

Zilinskas, Raymond A., "The Threat of Bioterrorism," Center for Nonproliferation Studies briefing, August 3, 1998, available at http://cns.miis.edu/iiop/cnsdata.

Zvi, Shabatai, "Israeli Settlers Destroy 17,000 Tons of Grapes," *Al-Ayyam*, October 23, 1997, available at http://www.hebron.com/article04-10-23-97.html.